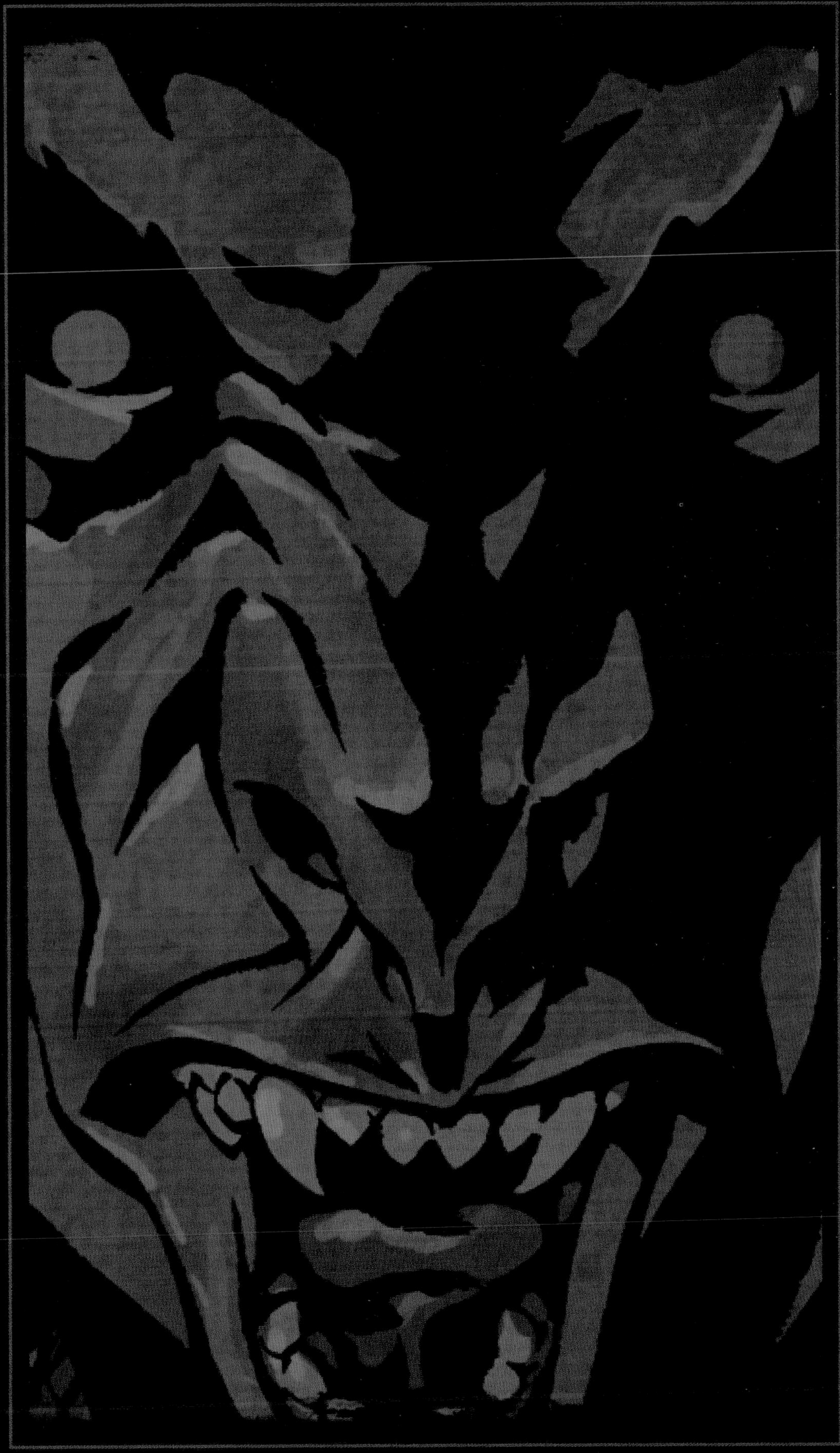

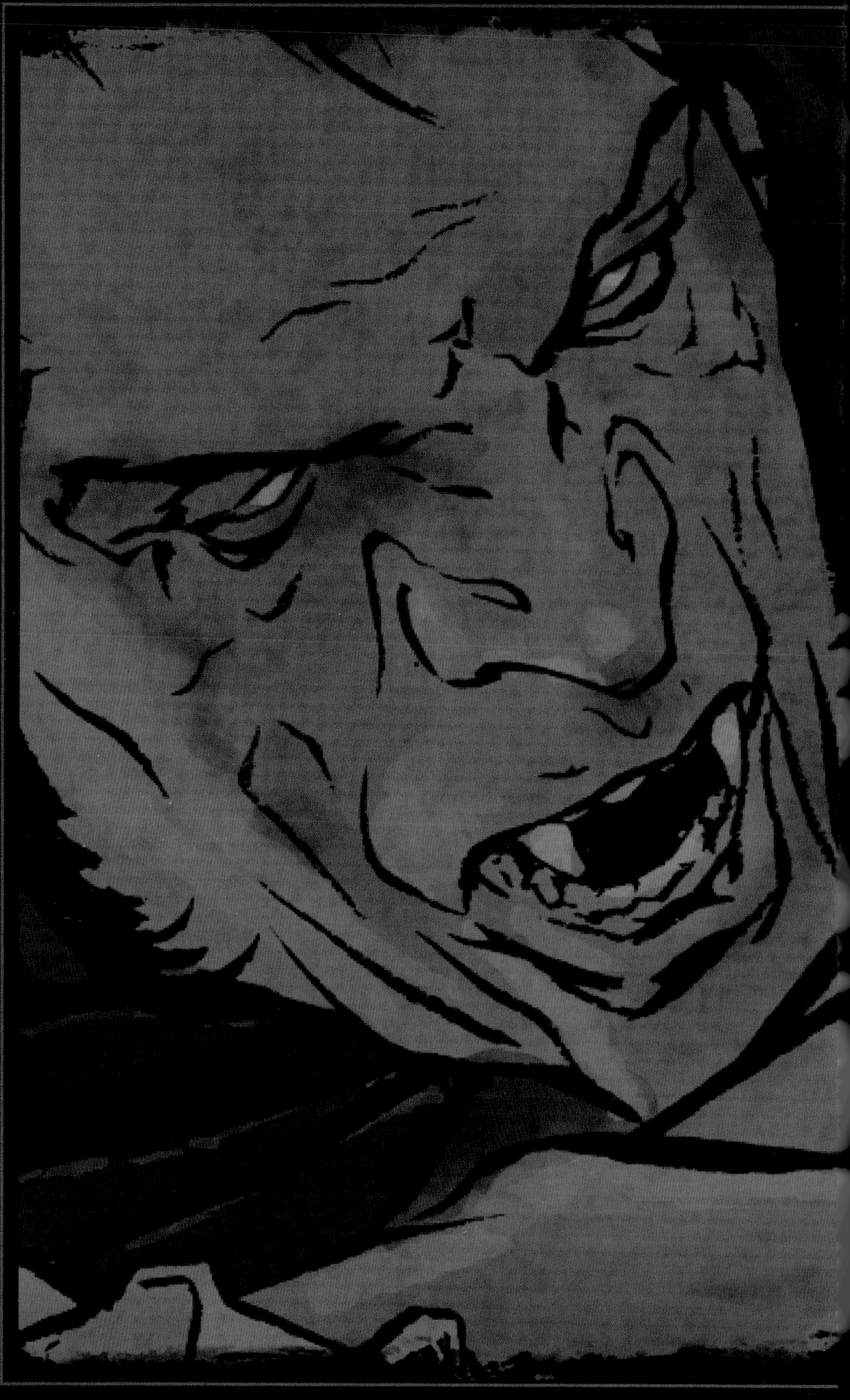

SHERLOCK HOLMES
AND THE VAMPIRES OF LONDON

Story by
SYLVAIN CORDURIÉ

Art by
LACI

Colors by
AXEL GONZALBO

Cover by
JEAN-SÉBASTIEN ROSSBACH

DARK HORSE BOOKS

Editor DANIEL CHABON

Designer AMY ARENDTS

President and Publisher MIKE RICHARDSON

Translated by LUMAX STUDIOS

Special thanks to Thierry Mornet

Neil Hankerson executive vice president · Tom Weddle chief financial officer · Randy Stradley vice president of publishing · Michael Martens vice president of book trade sales · Anita Nelson vice president of business affairs · Scott Allie editor in chief · Matt Parkinson vice president of marketing · David Scroggy vice president of product development · Dale LaFountain vice president of information technology Darlene Vogel senior director of print, design, and production · Ken Lizzi general counsel · Davey Estrada editorial director · Chris Warner senior books editor · Diana Schutz executive editor · Cary Grazzini director of print and development · Lia Ribacchi art director · Cara Niece director of scheduling · Tim Wiesch director of international licensing · Mark Bernardi director of digital publishing

Published by Dark Horse Books
A division of Dark Horse Comics, Inc.
10956 SE Main Street
Milwaukie, OR 97222

First edition: January 2014
ISBN 978-1-61655-266-4

10 9 8 7 6 5 4 3 2 1
Printed in China

International Licensing: (503) 905-2377
Comic Shop Locator Service: (888) 266-4226

This volume collects *Sherlock Holmes and the Vampires of London* Books 1 and 2, originally published by Soleil Productions.

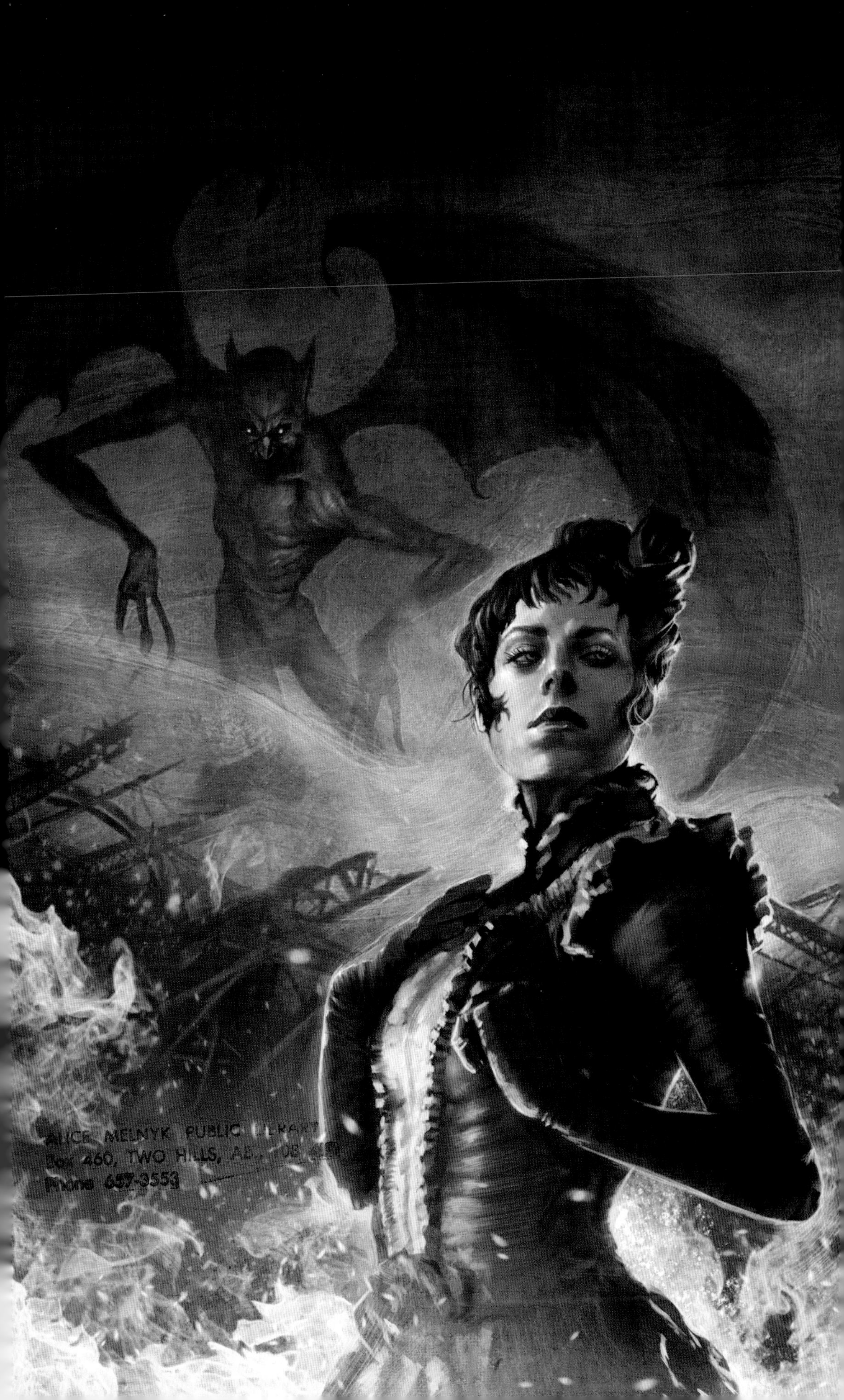

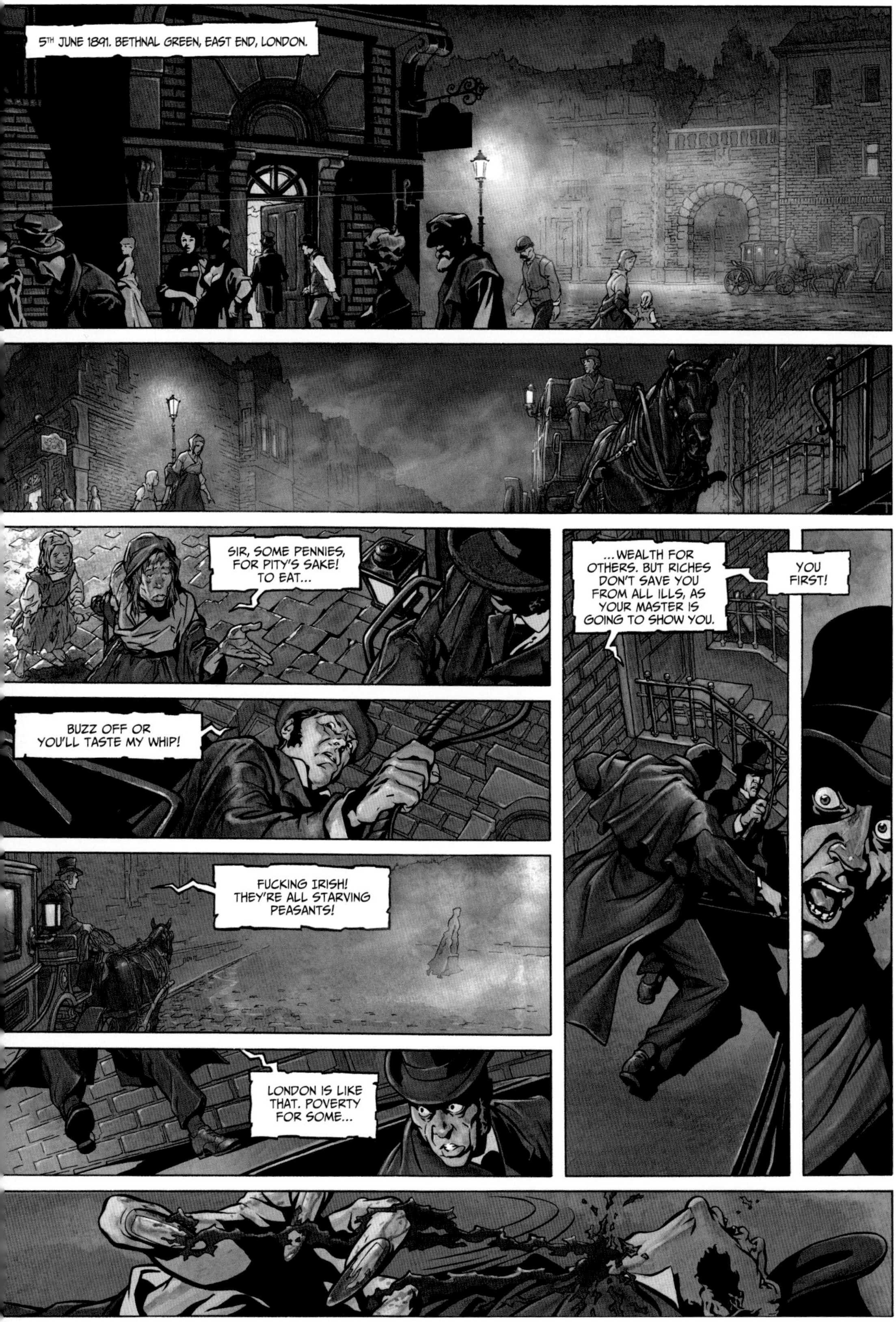
5TH JUNE 1891. BETHNAL GREEN, EAST END, LONDON.
SIR, SOME PENNIES, FOR PITY'S SAKE! TO EAT...
BUZZ OFF OR YOU'LL TASTE MY WHIP!
FUCKING IRISH! THEY'RE ALL STARVING PEASANTS!
LONDON IS LIKE THAT. POVERTY FOR SOME...
...WEALTH FOR OTHERS. BUT RICHES DON'T SAVE YOU FROM ALL ILLS, AS YOUR MASTER IS GOING TO SHOW YOU.
YOU FIRST!

TELL ME THAT YOU LIKE IT!

TELL ME!

YOU WANT SOME MORE, IS THAT IT?

KLAKK

I'M GOING TO STOP YOU FROM MAKING ME REPEAT MYSELF.

YOU TOLD ME-- THE LONGER I LAST, THE MORE YOU PAY ME...

SHUT UP, YOU BITCH! YOU'RE SPOILING EVERYTHING!

WHAT THE DEVIL--?!

THE DEVIL... NO, BUT YOU'LL SOON BE MEETING HIM.

...LORD BATTENKEY.

THROOW

AAAAHHHH!

SCREAM ALL YOU WANT!

I'VE GOT RID OF THE ONLY PERSON LIKELY TO HELP YOU.

YOU'RE ALL MINE!

COVINGTON, 1ST JULY 1891.

I HAVE NEVER BELIEVED IN CHANCE OR THE FORCE OF DESTINY.

AND YET I MUST ADMIT THAT HISTORY REPEATS ITSELF STRANGELY. TONIGHT, I SHALL BE FACING AGAIN FEARSOME ADVERSARIES.

I'VE PREPARED MYSELF FOR THIS MOMENT, JUST AS I PREPARED MYSELF TO CONFRONT PROFESSOR MORIARTY LAST MAY.

BUT THIS TIME, EVEN I WOULDN'T BET ON MY CHANCES OF COMING OUT OF IT ALIVE.

WATSON, YOU HAVE WRITTEN ABOUT ALL MY ADVENTURES.

NOW I MUST WRITE ABOUT THIS ONE, WITH THE CERTAINTY THAT, ALAS, I MAY NOT FINISH IT. BUT AS MY ALLY IS GIVING HIMSELF SOME HOURS OF REST...

...I'VE SOME HOURS TO KILL, IF YOU WILL EXCUSE THE PUN.

MIGHT AS WELL DO SOME USEFUL WORK.

THIS STORY BEGAN ONLY TWENTY DAYS AGO...

NAPOLEON III SQUARE, PARIS...

...ON JUNE 12TH, PRECISELY. MORE THAN A MONTH HAD PASSED SINCE MY "OFFICIAL" DEATH.

THE SWISS PRESS HAD RELATED THE CIRCUMSTANCES OF MY DEMISE IN THE REICHENBACH FALLS.

AND I DIDN'T DO ANYTHING TO REFUTE THAT VERSION OF THE FACTS.

MY RETURN TO PARIS CAME NATURALLY. I HAD OCCASIONALLY STAYED THERE FOR PROFESSIONAL REASONS. I HAD MY BEARINGS...

I THOUGHT THAT FOR ONCE MYCROFT WOULD ACCEPT TO BREAK UP HIS BELOVED ROUTINE.

BOULEVARD DES ITALIENS.

YES, SIR.

TO SHARE MY SECRET SHOULD REALLY EXCITE HIM, AND OUR REUNION EVEN MORE SO.

YOU DIDN'T TELL ME THAT YOU WOULD COME TO GET ME IN PERSON, SHERLOCK. DID YOU REALLY THINK YOU COULD FOIL ME WITH THIS DISGUISE?

MYCROFT ISN'T AN EXPANSIVE PERSON, BUT I FELT A NOTE OF EMOTION IN HIS VOICE.

NO. I WANTED TO MAKE SURE THAT YOU WEREN'T FOLLOWED, WITHOUT TAKING THE RISK OF BEING RECOGNIZED.

AND?

I DIDN'T SEE ANYTHING.

BELIEVE ME, I WAS REALLY PRUDENT-- VERY PRUDENT!

AS YOU PRESUMED, YOUR BAKER STREET HOME IS WATCHED BY MORIARTY'S FOLLOWERS. THEY DIDN'T BELIEVE IN YOUR DEATH.

IT WAS TO BE EXPECTED. I SHAN'T SEE LONDON AGAIN FOR A WHILE. ANY PROBLEMS WITH THE BANK?

NONE. YOUR MONEY IS IN MY BAG...

EXCELLENT!

NOW, LET ME RETURN THIS VICTORIA TO ITS OWNER AND FIND MY FACE AGAIN...

"...AND I SHALL INVITE YOU TO TASTE THE BEST FOIE GRAS IN TOWN!"

WATSON CAN'T GET OVER YOUR DEATH. ACCORDING TO MRS. HUDSON, HE FEELS PARTLY RESPONSIBLE FOR IT.

I'M SORRY TO HEAR THAT, BUT I THINK THAT IT IS FOR THE BEST.

WATSON IS A POOR ACTOR.

IF HE KNEW ABOUT ME, HE COULDN'T STOP HIMSELF FROM SHOWING SIGNS.

HIS GRIEF WILL CONVINCE MY ENEMIES THAT HE KNOWS NOTHING. IT IS BY FAR HIS BEST PROTECTION.

WELL... TELL ME WHAT YOU ARE THINKING OF DOING, APART FROM ABAN-DONING YOURSELF TO THE JOYS OF FRENCH GASTRONOMY?

TRAVELING. IT'S A PROJECT THAT I'VE OFTEN DELAYED.

SHERLOCK...

I WAS TOO BUSY TO ENVISAGE IT SERIOUSLY. I NOW HAVE THE CHANCE TO TAKE THE PLUNGE.

...THERE IS A SUBJECT THAT I MUST BRING UP. I KNOW THAT WATSON HAD LITTLE AUTHORITY OVER YOU, BUT YOU LISTENED TO HIM, EVEN SO.

13

WITHOUT HIM BESIDE YOU, I'M AFRAID THAT YOU WILL GIVE IN TO YOUR TENDENCIES...

MY DEAR BROTHER, IT IS VERY HONORABLE OF YOU TO WORRY ABOUT MY AUGUST PERSON!

BUT IF I LISTENED TO THE VOICE OF REASON, YOU WOULD KNOW IT, WOULDN'T YOU?

I CAN, HOWEVER, REASSURE YOU THAT I HAVE DONE WITHOUT STIMULANTS SINCE I LEFT ENGLAND. IN TRUTH, I'M THE FIRST PERSON SURPRISED.

HOWEVER UNPLEASANT MY SITUATION IS, IT APPEARS TO HAVE A BENEFICIAL EFFECT.

MY INTELLECT IS BEING CALLED UPON AS RARELY BEFORE.

MY MIND IS CONSTANTLY BOILING OVER. IT'S SO EXHILARATING!

I SHALL USE MY CONNECTION TO GET RID OF MORIARTY'S UNDERLINGS. YOU CAN COUNT ON ME.

COME! MY NEW LANDLADY IS FROM BIRMINGHAM AND DOESN'T OFTEN HAVE THE OCCASION OF RECEIVING HER MAJESTY'S SUBJECTS.

BE PATIENT, MYCROFT... BELIEVE ME, THEY ARE NOT STUPID.

WHEN I TOLD HER THAT MY BROTHER WOULD VISIT ME, SHE MADE ME PROMISE TO INTRODUCE YOU TO HER.

I OWE HER THIS FAVOR. SHE HAS BEEN RATHER ACCOMMODATING TO ME.

HERE WE ARE!

YOU'LL SEE, MRS. IRBY IS A CHARMING LADY...

MAYBE SHE FORGOT TO SHUT THE DOOR.

NOT VERY LIKELY.

HER DOOR HAS MORE LOCKS THAN HINGES.

HOW COULD I HAVE IMAGINED WHAT HER MURDERER REALLY WAS?

HER BLOOD HAD A SUGARY TASTE. HOW PLEASANT...

I NOTICED IMMEDIATELY HER PALLOR AND THE MARKS ON HER NECK. WAS THIS A SINISTER SETUP?

MYCROFT! GET BACK!

WHERE TO?

THE GREAT SHERLOCK HOLMES... WHO IS NAIVE ENOUGH TO BELIEVE HE CAN DISAPPEAR FROM EVERYONE'S VIEW.

MY MASTER WANTS YOU TO JOIN US. HE HAS PLANS FOR YOU.

IF YOU WOULD DO ME THE FAVOR OF CRANING YOUR NECK...

VAMPIRES!

I WAS UNDER THE SHOCK OF THIS DISCOVERY WHEN THE CREATURE ATTACKED. I ACTED BY REFLEX.

ONCE AGAIN, MY YEARS PRACTICING JUJITSU WERE OF GREAT USE.

MYCROFT DIDN'T HAVE THE SAME MEANS OF DEFENSE.

ALAS, HE HAD TO MANAGE BY HIMSELF... SINCE I WAS TOO BUSY.

CLAKK

I DO PREFER FRENCH FOOD, BUT ONE MUST TASTE EVERYTHING TO BE SURE!

YAAHH!

WE SHALL MEET AGAIN, HOLMES!

LET ME DEAL WITH THAT!

WE MANAGED TO DODGE THE POLICE. I COULDN'T ALLOW MYSELF TO BE QUESTIONED AND THUS RUIN ALL MY EFFORTS IN MAKING PEOPLE BELIEVE IN MY DEATH. ALSO, I HAD TO LOOK AFTER MYCROFT.

HIS HANDS WERE SEVERELY BURNED AND HE HAD TO BE HIDDEN. ONCE A DOCTOR HAD GIVEN HIM THE NECESSARY TREATMENT...

...I SENT HIM TO MY FRIEND INSPECTOR DUBUQUE. IN THE RECENT PAST, I HAD HELPED HIM TO SOLVE A STATE AFFAIR. HE'D PROMISED ME HELP IF NEEDED.

HE WOULD DO ME THE "POSTHUMOUS" FAVOR OF PROTECTING MY BROTHER, WHOM I ADVISED TO LIE ON THE NATURE OF OUR ATTACKERS. AT THE BEST, THEY'D THINK HIM MAD.

WITH MYCROFT OUT OF DANGER, I COULD CONCENTRATE ON THE VAMPIRES. THEIR EXISTENCE SHOULD HAVE TERRIFIED ME, BUT CURIOSITY WAS TAKING OVER...

I, WHO HAD NEVER BELIEVED IN THE SUPERNATURAL, WENT IN SEARCH OF THE WRITINGS OF PROFESSOR ABRAHAM VAN HELSING...

...AND CONSULTED THE WORKS HE REFERRED TO.

SOME WERE SO SPECIALIZED THAT I HAD TO CONSULT PRIVATE COLLECTIONS.

I LEARNT ENOUGH ABOUT THESE MONSTERS TO KNOW HOW TO DEFEND MYSELF IN THE CASE OF A NEW ATTACK. THEY HADN'T TRIED TO KILL ME. THEY JUST WANTED ME TO SHARE THEIR CONDITION.

THEY THEREFORE NEEDED ME. MY ACTION WAS GOING TO FOLLOW THIS CONCLUSION. IF I JUDGED CORRECTLY, OF WHICH I HAD NO DOUBT, I HAD ACES TO PLAY...

HAVING OPENED A BANK ACCOUNT UNDER THE IDENTITY OF MAGNUS SIGERSON, AND PAID FOR MRS. IRBY'S FUNERAL...

...I PUT MY PLAN INTO ACTION. AS THE VAMPIRES WERE LOOKING FOR ME, I WAS GOING TO DO MY BEST TO FACILITATE THE TASK FOR THEM.

I WENT TO ALL THE PLACES THAT I USED TO GO TO. I DIDN'T HAVE TO WAIT FOR LONG.

I HAD UNDERESTIMATED THEM. THEY KNEW ME BETTER THAN I HAD THOUGHT.

ENOUGH TO USE THIS AMAZING DOUBLE OF IRENE ADLER!

BUT THE STRATAGEM THEY USED SURPRISED ME.

THAT THEY WERE USING HER WAS BOTH CRUEL AND INGENIOUS! I DIDN'T DISAPPOINT THEM...

THEN, NOT WITHOUT APPREHENSION, I PREPARED MYSELF TO ENTER THE WOLF'S LAIR.

...AND FOLLOWED WITH FASCINATION THIS UNSURPASSED MODEL OF FEMININITY.

I HESITATED A MOMENT... THERE WOULD BE NO GOING BACK...

HE DIDN'T MAKE A SOUND BUT, ALL THE SAME, I FELT HIM SLIPPING UP TO MY BACK.

IT WAS THE MOMENT OF TRUTH...

HOLMES, I WAS EAGER TO MEET YOU AGAIN...

IT SEEMS THAT YOU CAN BE AS EASILY MANIPULATED AS THE MOST COMMON OF MORTALS.

DON'T YOU KNOW THAT IRENE ADLER DIED TWO YEARS AGO?

IT IS TRUE THAT AFTER SHE HAD OUTSMARTED YOU, SHE SUDDENLY LEFT ENGLAND FOR THE CONTINENT.

YOU FOILED ME ONCE, HOLMES. I WILL HAVE MY REVENGE BY READING THE FEAR IN YOUR EYES.

WE MUSTN'T DAMAGE HIM, STINFIELD!

YOU'RE RIGHT...

HE IS PRECIOUS TO THE EYES OF SELYMES.

I'LL JUST HALF EMPTY HIM!

AKKH?!

ARRRRHHHH!

STINFIELD!

WHAT HAVE YOU DONE, YOU SON OF A BITCH?

WHAT ANY WISE MAN SHOULD DO. I'VE DEVELOPED A TASTE FOR HOLY WATER.

OF COURSE, YOU COULD KILL ME. YOU'RE DYING TO. BUT YOU WON'T.

AS YOUR DEAD COMPANION REMINDED YOU, YOUR MASTER NEEDS ME.

LET HIM GO, GERALD!

WHEN DO WE LEAVE?

TOMORROW. FOR CALAIS.

I CAME TO YOU OF MY OWN FREE WILL, AND I DON'T INTEND TO ESCAPE FROM YOU.

IF YOUR MASTER WANTS ME, I'M READY TO MEET HIM. BUT IT WILL BE AS A MAN AND NOT A MONSTER THAT I SHALL PRESENT MYSELF TO HIM.

IN THE MEANTIME, YOU ARE MY GUEST, MR. HOLMES.

THE PAS-DE-CALAIS STRAITS.

I QUICKLY REALIZED THAT THE VAMPIRE COMMUNITY, BECAUSE THERE WAS ONE, HAD MANY HUMAN SERVANTS.

AND ALMOST UNLIMITED MEANS. HIRING A SHIP WAS A MERE FORMALITY.

YOU KNEW SHE WAS DEAD, DIDN'T YOU?

I LEARNT IT FROM A FRIEND WHO LIVED IN THE SAME TOWN AS SHE AND WHO WENT TO THE SAME DINNERS.

AS SHE WAS A REMARKABLE WOMAN, THE ANNOUNCEMENT OF HER DEATH SHOOK THE SOCIETY SHE HONORED BY HER PRESENCE.

WHEN THE NEWS REACHED ME, I WAS SO SHOCKED THAT I REMAINED PROSTRATE FOR THREE DAYS.

I DON'T THINK THAT I'VE CONSUMED AS MANY DRUGS AS DURING THAT PERIOD.

IT MADE THE SITUATION EASIER TO BEAR.

YOU LOVED HER THAT MUCH?

I COULDN'T SAY, BUT KNOWING THAT SHE HAS GONE CREATES A VACUUM THAT NOTHING WILL EVER FILL.

NOT EVEN A COPY, HOWEVER PERFECT IT IS.

MY NAME IS JOYCE MIDDLES.

DON'T YOU FEEL HATE TOWARDS THOSE WHO HAVE STOLEN YOUR LIFE?

MY LIFE...

SINCE WE ARE CONFIDING IN EACH OTHER, THERE IS A POINT THAT I SHOULD LIKE TO BRING UP WITH YOU, IF YOU WILL ALLOW ME. YOU ARE INTELLIGENT. YOU CANNOT IGNORE THE FACT THAT IT WAS ONLY TO TRAP ME THAT THEY MADE YOU A VAMPIRE.

IF YOU ONLY KNEW HOW BLEAK IT WAS.

BY LOSING IT, I GAINED ETERNITY, A WIDER PERCEPTION OF THE WORLD, MORE INTENSE SENSATIONS...

AND AN UNQUENCHABLE THIRST THAT FORCES YOU TO COMMIT BARBARIC CRIMES. DOESN'T THAT AFFECT YOU?

I DON'T FEEL REMORSE ANY LONGER.

AND, UNLIKE YOU, THE EMPTINESS OF MY EXISTENCE HAS GIVEN WAY TO ACCOMPLISHMENT... TO A FEELING OF FULLNESS.

AM I, OF US TWO, TO BE PITIED MORE?

THE NEXT DAY AT CHARING CROSS STATION, LONDON.

SO, I HAD MADE A MISTAKE IN MY FORECAST.

I WAS BACK IN LONDON. CERTAINLY NOT IN IDEAL CONDITIONS, BUT MY NATURE IS SUCH THAT I SAVORED THE MOMENT.

FROM NOW ON, WE SHALL CONSTANTLY KEEP AN EYE ON YOU.

I CAN SEE THAT.

REALLY?

I HAVE ALREADY NOTICED THREE MEN MAKING SUCH EFFORTS TO PASS UNNOTICED THAT ONE CAN'T MISS THEM.

STINFIELD PAID DEARLY FOR UNDERESTIMATING YOU, HOLMES. YOU MUST KNOW THAT WE SHALL NOT MAKE THE SAME MISTAKE.

I WOULD BE SURPRISED IF THEY WERE BETTER AT TAILING ME, BUT YOU CAN BE SURE THAT I DON'T INTEND TO ESCAPE FROM THEM.

PERLISS CLUB.

JOHN, YOU SHOULD PERHAPS STOP THERE.

NOT THAT I MIND TAKING YOUR MONEY, BUT IT IS OBVIOUSLY NOT YOUR EVENING TONIGHT.

LUCK MAY CHANGE, SIR YARBROUGH.

AND SOMETHING TELLS ME THAT IT WILL HAPPEN SOON.

ANOTHER OF YOUR FAMOUS INTUITIONS, MY BOY?

FOR YOUR WALLET'S SAKE, MAYBE IT WOULD BE WISER TO IGNORE IT.

THINK OF POOR PATRICK! EVERY TIME HE BAILS YOU OUT, HIS FORTUNE MELTS LIKE SNOW IN THE SUN.

DON'T WORRY ABOUT ME, BLAKE. THE ICEBERG IS BIG ENOUGH.

EVEN IF JOHN AND I SHOULD ACCUMULATE THE LOSING HANDS, MY VULTURES OF DESCENDANTS WILL STILL HAVE QUITE ENOUGH TO GLUT THEMSELVES ON.

WELL, I WOULD HAVE DONE EVERYTHING TO STOP THE HEMORR--

KRAKKK

27

IS THAT THE PUBLIC MENACE EMERSON AGAIN? WHEN WILL THE CIRCLE DECIDE TO EXCLUDE HIM?

HE'S ONE OF THE MOST DANGEROUS DRUNKS. I CAN'T UNDERSTAND WHY THEY STILL SERVE HIM DRIN--

I HAVE COME FOR JOHN SOMERSETT.

THE SAME SMELL AS YOUR FATHER... AND SOON THE SMELL OF CARRION...

GOOD LORD!

CREATURE OF THE DEVIL! DON'T COME NEAR ME!

I'M NOT AFTER YOU BUT, IF YOU INSIST, I'M NOT FUSSY ABOUT MORE CORPSES.

WE'RE GETTING CLOSE. IF YOUR CURIOSITY GETS THE BETTER OF YOU, YOU CAN LOOK OUT.

I FELT UNEASY EVEN BEFORE SEEING THE CASTLE.

AS IF NEARING A MAGNETIC EVIL, ITS DARKNESS ATTRACTED ME AND WEIGHED UPON ME AT THE SAME TIME.

THE FEELING INCREASED AS WE NEARED IT.

PART OF ME CRIED OUT THAT I HAD TO FLEE THIS PLACE. BUT ANOTHER PART OF ME FELT AN INDESCRIBABLE EXCITEMENT...

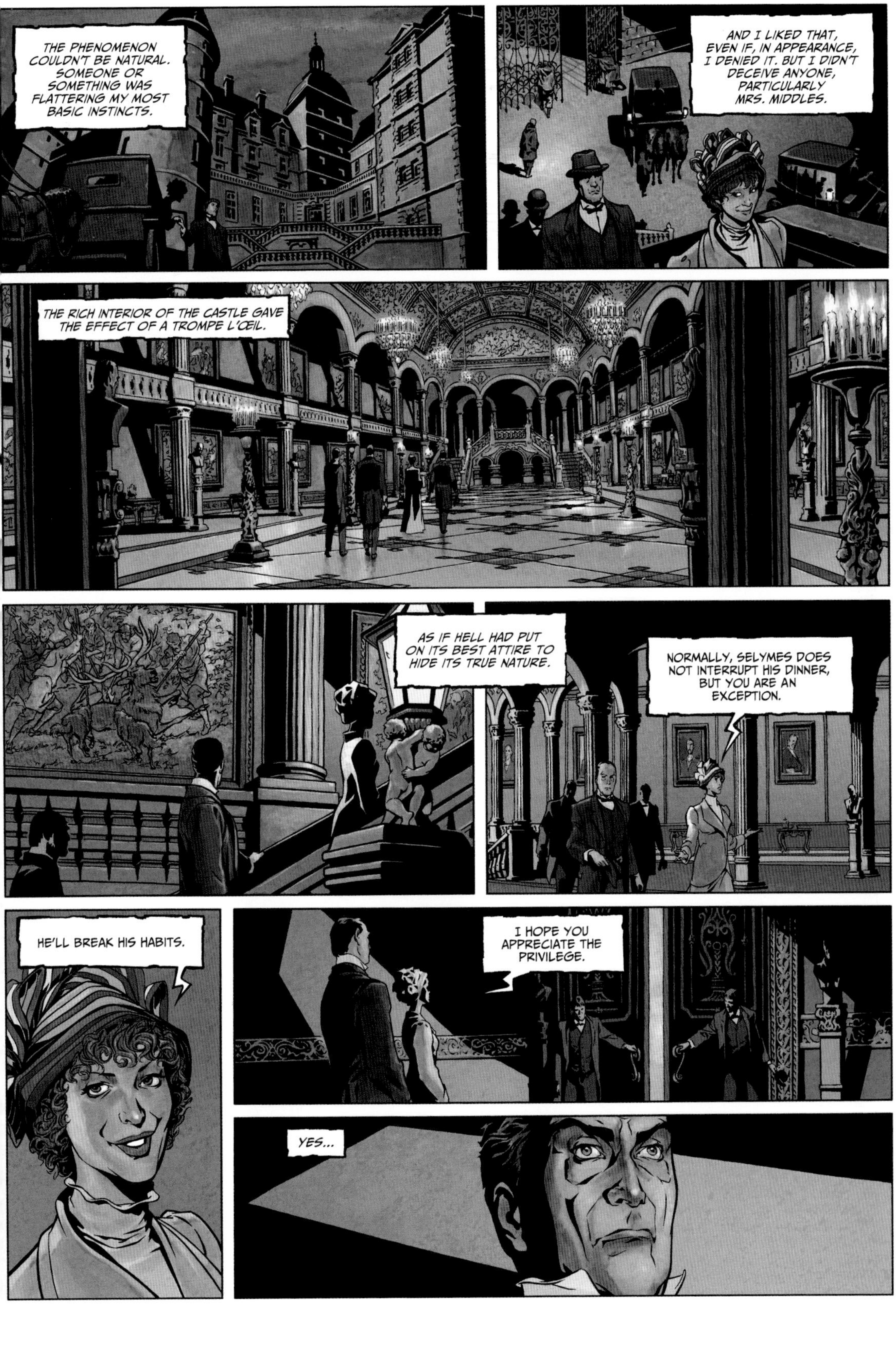
THE PHENOMENON COULDN'T BE NATURAL. SOMEONE OR SOMETHING WAS FLATTERING MY MOST BASIC INSTINCTS.
AND I LIKED THAT, EVEN IF, IN APPEARANCE, I DENIED IT. BUT I DIDN'T DECEIVE ANYONE, PARTICULARLY MRS. MIDDLES.
THE RICH INTERIOR OF THE CASTLE GAVE THE EFFECT OF A TROMPE L'ŒIL.
AS IF HELL HAD PUT ON ITS BEST ATTIRE TO HIDE ITS TRUE NATURE.
NORMALLY, SELYMES DOES NOT INTERRUPT HIS DINNER, BUT YOU ARE AN EXCEPTION.
HE'LL BREAK HIS HABITS.
I HOPE YOU APPRECIATE THE PRIVILEGE.
YES...

...HELL DID EXIST...

YOU'RE CONTROLLING YOURSELF REMARKABLY, HOLMES. MANY WOULD PASS OUT BEFORE THIS SPECTACLE.

I'VE BEEN TOLD HOW YOU GOT RID OF STINFIELD. SIMPLE, EFFECTIVE, AND CLEVER.

WHAT A PITY YOU REFUSE TO BE BITTEN! YOU WOULD BE A MORE REFINED COMPANION THAN MOST OF THE BRUTES WHO SURROUND ME.

THE PLEASURE WOULD BE ONLY YOURS. I MYSELF FIND YOU REPUGNANT.

LOOKING AT YOU, DYING DOESN'T SEEM SO DRAMATIC.

YOU'RE TREADING A VERY RISKY PATH, HOLMES. I COULD TEACH YOU A THOUSAND PAINS FOR SUCH INSOLENCE.

NGHHH!

AGGHH!

A PROBLEM? YOUR ENTRAILS ARE CONTRACTING, PERHAPS?

WHAT LESSON HAVE YOU TO GIVE ME, YOU PITIFUL COCAINE ADDICT? YOU, WHO DEBASE YOURSELF IN A SELF-DESTRUCTING DEPENDENCY!

AT... LEAST... I CHOOSE... MY DAMNATION!

NOW... SINCE WE BOTH KNOW... THAT YOU WILL NOT TAKE MY LIFE AWAY... TELL ME WHY... I AM HERE...

AAAHHH...

BREATHE SLOWLY... THE PAIN WILL GO AWAY...

A FEW YEARS AGO, ONE OF MY PROTÉGÉS CONTRACTED A DEGENERATIVE ILLNESS. HE COULDN'T CONTROL HIMSELF, BECAME AGGRESSIVE...

AFTER HE HAD COMMITTED SEVERAL SAVAGE MURDERS WHICH ATTRACTED ATTENTION TO US, WE FINALLY CAPTURED HIM.

OWEN CHANES--THAT'S HIS NAME-- STAYED IMPRISONED FOR A LONG TIME TO MEDITATE ON HIS CRIMES, UNTIL SOME FOOL LET HIM ESCAPE.

HATING US, HE DECIDED TO ATTACK INFLUENTIAL PEOPLE, TO KILL AGAIN AND AGAIN IN ORDER TO DESTROY THE MUTUALLY PROFITABLE RELATIONSHIPS THAT WE HAVE WITH THE ESTABLISHMENT.

AND HE SUCCEEDED. QUEEN VICTORIA HERSELF ORDERED US TO GET RID OF HIM AS SOON AS POSSIBLE, OR WE WOULD BE EXTERMINATED.

THE PROBLEM IS THAT CHANES IS CLEVER AND ELUSIVE.

IF WE HAD TIME, WE COULD CAPTURE HIM...

...BUT TIME IS PRECISELY WHAT WE'RE LACKING.

AS PART OF OUR ACTIVITIES, WE COLLABORATE WITH ALL TYPES OF CRIMINALS, AND PARTICULARLY WITH MORIARTY'S GANG.

WE LEARNT THROUGH THEM THAT YOU WERE STILL OF THIS WORLD. IT WAS EASY TO FIND YOU. THE LIVING LEAVE SO MANY TRACES...

WHY SHOULD I HELP YOU? IT'S OBVIOUS AFTER ALL THESE REVELATIONS THAT YOU WON'T LET ME LIVE.

AND THE EVENTUALITY THAT YOU WOULD BE PERSECUTED QUITE PLEASES ME...

WE COULD CAUSE A LOT OF PROB- LEMS BEFORE DISAPPEARING.

SH RAAAKK

DO YOU THINK THAT MARY WATSON'S SKELETON IS MORE RESISTANT?

IT WAS TIME TO TELL HIM WHAT HE WANTED TO HEAR.

IF I HELP YOU, I WANT YOUR WORD THAT NONE OF MY CLOSE FRIENDS WILL BE BOTHERED IN ANY WAY WHATSOEVER.

IF YOU ELIMINATE CHANES.

HE'S STRUCK AGAIN!

I'LL NEED A PICTURE OF THIS MAN, A CHEMICAL LABORATORY, AND SUBSTANTIAL FUNDS...

SELYMES... DANGELD ASKS TO BE ADMITTED.

WHAT IS IT? YOU KNOW THAT I DON'T WANT TO BE INTERRUPTED.

IT'S CHANES, MASTER.

HOLMES?

THE SIGHT OF BLOOD...

IT'S A FASCINATION THAT YOU CANNOT REPROACH ME FOR, MRS. MIDDLES, YOU'LL AGREE...

HURRY UP! I CAN'T HOLD UP THE SCOTLAND YARD PEOPLE FOREVER!

DO QUICKLY WHAT YOU HAVE TO DO, AND THEN LET'S LEAVE THIS WALKING CEMETERY!

FORGIVE MY DAYDREAMING, MR.-- CARDY, IS THAT RIGHT?

CHANES CAME FOR SOMERSETT.

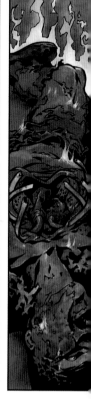

HE'S THE ILLEGITIMATE SON OF A MEMBER OF THE ROYAL FAMILY.

HE'S CRUSHED HIS HEART.

HE DID THE SAME WITH HIS OTHER VICTIMS.

BY ATTACKING ROYALTY, EVEN INDIRECTLY, HE'S CLIMBED ANOTHER ECHELON.

HOW MANY HAS HE KILLED?

IF WE INCLUDE SOMERSETT, HIS HUNTING TROPHIES ARE EIGHT CROSSES.

HE WOUNDED HIS MURDERER.

SO?

THE BLOOD ON THIS POKER CAN GIVE PRECIOUS INFORMATION TO EXPERT HANDS.

WE CAN GO, MR. CARDY.

CHANES DIDN'T WORRY ABOUT THE CLUES HE LEFT BEHIND HIM, AND DIDN'T ENCUMBER HIMSELF WITH DETAILS. THAT'S IDEAL FOR A DETECTIVE.

AMONGST THE MEMBERS OF SCOTLAND YARD KICKING THEIR HEELS ABOUT IN FRONT OF THE CLUB, I SAW MY FRIEND INSPECTOR LESTRADE.

FOR HIS OWN SAFETY, I COULD NOT ALLOW HIM TO SEE ME.

I KNEW THAT THE CLUB MEMBERS WOULD BE FORCED TO KEEP SILENT, IN A DEFINITIVE MANNER IF NECESSARY, AND THE SCOTLAND YARD DETECTIVES WOULD NEVER HAND IN THEIR CONCLUSIONS.

SELYMES HAD HAD A LABORATORY INSTALLED IN THE HOUSE WHERE I WAS LIVING DURING THE ENQUIRY.

IT WOULD HAVE BEEN MORE SENSIBLE TO FINISH THE NIGHT WITH A FEW HOURS OF SLEEP, BUT I WANTED THE BLOOD TO GIVE UP ITS SECRETS.

OF COURSE, MY ANALYSES DIDN'T AIM AT FACILITATING CHANES'S CAPTURE. I WANTED ABOVE ALL TO FURTHER MY KNOWLEDGE OF VAMPIRES.

AND TO DISCOVER THEIR WEAK POINTS.

ALAS, ALL I LEARNT WAS THAT THEIR BLOOD DOES NOT COAGULATE AND THAT IT IS PARTICULARLY VISCOUS, A DEFENSE SYSTEM AGAINST HEMORRHAGES.

THE NEXT DAY, I STARTED TO FULFILL MY PART OF THE ENGAGEMENT.

I CALLED ON THE SERVICES OF INFORMERS, SHOWING THEM ETCHINGS OF CHANES. A PHOTOGRAPH WOULD HAVE BEEN MORE ACCURATE BUT, ACCORDING TO SELYMES, THERE WEREN'T ANY.

BUT RATHER THAN CHASING CHANES, I OPTED FOR A MORE PRODUCTIVE APPROACH...

MY MESSAGE WAS SIMPLE: I WAS LOOKING FOR OWEN CHANES AND WOULD PAY A LARGE SUM OF MONEY FOR INFORMATION.

I CHOSE INDISCREET PEOPLE SO THAT CHANES WOULD KNOW THAT I WAS MOVING HEAVEN AND EARTH TO FIND HIM.

I ALSO WANTED THE VIGILANCE OF MY CHAPERONES TO RELAX LITTLE BY LITTLE. TO DO SO, I INSTALLED THEM IN A ROUTINE THAT WOULD BEAR FRUIT LATER ON.

AFTER TWO DAYS, NEWS THAT MR. SIGERSON WAS TRACKING A CERTAIN CHANES HAD SPREAD THROUGH THE TOWN.

I GAVE A SINGLE MEETING POINT TO MY EVENTUAL INFORMERS.

EVERY EVENING I DINED IN THE SAME ITALIAN RESTAURANT WITH MY WIFE, MRS. SIGERSON.

YOU'RE NOT EATING?

THAT WILL COME... LATER.

TO FEED HER, SOMEONE HAD TO DIE TONIGHT. BUT I COULDN'T DO ANYTHING, AT LEAST FOR THE TIME BEING.

YOU ARE A MYSTERY, MR. HOLMES.

YOU HAVE SHOWN UNRESERVED SCORN FOR OUR RACE, AND YET YOU HAVE MADE A PACT WITH MY MASTER ON THE BASIS OF A WORD OF HONOR.

HOW CAN YOU BE SURE THAT HE WILL RESPECT THIS MORAL CONTRACT?

BODY LANGUAGE. HE DOESN'T LIE.

SELYMES'S MANNERS LEAD ME TO BELIEVE THAT HE IS OF NOBLE BLOOD... PERHAPS A DUKE OR A COUNT.

HE DOESN'T SEEK TO HIDE HIS EMOTIONS. IT IS IMPORTANT TO HIM TO INSPIRE RESPECT AS MUCH AS FEAR. FOR THESE REASONS, AND FOR OTHERS, YES, I TRUST HIS WORD.

HE IS A DUKE...

DEDUCING IT WAS CHILD'S PLAY.

DO YOU REALLY THINK CHANES WILL SHOW UP?

IT IS EASIER TO BRING PEOPLE TO ONESELF THAN TO RUN AFTER THEM.

I AM COUNTING ON HIS CURIOSITY.

I PRESENT MY EXCUSES TO YOU, SUNS...

I'VE ALREADY SENT THE OTHER LOOKOUTS TO BURN IN HELL.

SUCH AS I KNOW YOU LOT, YOU MUST BE DYING TO JOIN THEM, AREN'T YOU? YOU ARE SUCH A CLOSE COMMUNITY...

REST ASSURED...

I DON'T HAVE THE INTENTION OF KEEPING YOU HERE MUCH LONGER.

I'M AFRAID THAT YOUR HOPES WILL BE DASHED AGAIN.

PATIENCE IS AN ESSENTIAL QUALITY IN MY PROFESSION.

IF CHANES DOESN'T SHOW UP TODAY, PERHAPS HE WILL TOMORROW.

KLING

SUNS!

YOU WERE RIGHT, HOLMES! BUT HE HAS BEEN CLEVERER THAN US. HE MUST BE FAR AWAY BY NOW.

I DON'T THINK SO. HE WANTS TO KNOW WHO IS AFTER HIM.

HE IS OUT THERE, SOMEWHERE.

SHERLOCK HOLMES...

SELYMES SUMMONED ME THE NEXT DAY.

ARE YOU AN ART LOVER, MR. HOLMES?

NOT REALLY.

THAT'S A PITY. YOU CLOSE YOURSELF TO A WORLD OF SENSUALITY.

LOOK AT THIS WORK BY CARAVAGGIO.

THE ANGEL MARY, DIVINE PERFECTION AND BESTIALITY... THIS ANIMAL PART THAT REASONABLE MEN LIKE YOU SPEND THEIR TIME SMOTHERING.

CARAVAGGIO GAVE HIMSELF UP TO WHAT HE WAS, WITHOUT HOLDING BACK, AND IT SHOWED IN HIS WORKS, JUST AS IN HIS LIFE.

NO ARTIST HAS BETTER DEFINED WHAT WE ARE.

IF HE HAD KNOWN YOU, PERHAPS HE WOULD HAVE BEEN MOTIVATED TO FIGHT HIS NATURE.

EVERYTHING IS A QUESTION OF CHOICE FOR YOU...

43

WHEN THERE IS A PREMEDITATED MURDER, YES.

CHANES SLIPPED BETWEEN YOUR FINGERS LAST NIGHT.

I WOULD RATHER SAY THAT YOUR MEN WERE CAUGHT UNAWARES. OTHERWISE HE WOULD HAVE BEEN AT YOUR MERCY.

I RECEIVED THIS PRESENT THIS MORNING. IT CONTAINS THE ASHES OF... MY LATE GOVERNMENT CONTACT.

A NOTE JOINED TO THE PARCEL SAID THAT OTHER BOXES ARE WAITING TO BE FILLED.

THE DEATH OF JOHN SOMERSETT HAS MADE QUEEN VICTORIA'S THREATS EVEN MORE... CONCRETE.

I SEE...

I DOUBT IT!

MY ROOM TO MANEUVER WAS GETTING DANGEROUSLY SMALL. AND I DIDN'T HAVE THE SLIGHTEST LEAD!

DO I HAVE TO MUTILATE YOUR FRIEND AND HIS WIFE TO GET SATISFACTION?

THERE WON'T BE ANY OTHER WARNING. SO, DEMONSTRATE YOUR TALENT WITHOUT WAITING ANY LONGER!

I WENT BACK TO THE CRIME SCENES, ENDING BY GASPERI'S. PERHAPS I WOULD COME ACROSS A DETAIL...

MY ADVERSARY WAS ANYTHING BUT STUPID. IF HE HAD MANAGED TO AVOID THE TRAP I'D SET HIM...

BUT I WAS UNDER NO ILLUSIONS. WHAT REVELATION COULD I EXPECT?

...I COULDN'T COUNT ON HIM MAKING A BIG MISTAKE. ALL THINGS CONSIDERED, I NOW HAD JUST TO WAIT FOR HIS NEXT ACTION.

I DIDN'T THINK IT WOULD HAPPEN SO SOON.

MISTER! I'VE SOMETHING FOR YOU!

WHO GAVE THAT TO YOU?

A CHAP PAID ME TEN POUNDS TO GIVE THIS TO YOU IN PERSON.

HE SAID THAT I'D SEE THE MAN DRAWN ON IT MESSING ABOUT IN THIS DISTRICT.

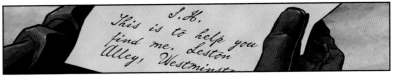

S.H.
This is to help you find me. Leston Alley, Westmins...

LATER.

WHERE'S HOLMES, CARDY?

AT THE END OF THE CUL-DE-SAC.

I'M WARNING YOU... IT'S NOT A PRETTY SIGHT, MRS. MIDDLES.

CARDY IDENTIFIED HIM. IT'S MARCUS STONE, A RETIRED GENERAL CLOSE TO THE QUEEN.

OUR KILLER SHOWS SINGLENESS OF PURPOSE.

INDEED.

S.H.?

YES, CHANES KNOWS ABOUT ME. BUT I'LL TAKE THAT INTO CONSIDERATION LATER.

HE DRANK STONE'S BLOOD BEFORE TEARING OFF HIS LIMBS.

HE'S GOING FURTHER AND FURTHER. TO MAKE THE QUEEN ACT AGAINST US.

YES, NO DOUBT. BUT WHY LEAD ME TO STONE? TO PROVOKE ME?

HAVE YOU FOUND SOMETHING?

NO, AND THE PLACE HAS BEEN CLEANED BY THE RAIN...

SO, THERE'S NO USE REMAINING UNDER THIS DELUGE.

SELYMES WOULD PUNISH ME IF YOU CAUGHT A FEVER.

YOU'RE WORRIED, HOLMES? IF YOU ARE ANTICIPATING SELYMES'S ANGER, YOU SHOULD BE...

IT'S SOMETHING ELSE...

CHANES HAS DECIDED TO LEAD THE DANCE. WHICH GIVES HIM AN ADVANCE IN TIME ON US.

WHAT CAN HE GAIN FROM IT?

IT'S NOT VERY IMPORTANT. STONE'S MURDER WILL PROBABLY HAVE CONSEQUENCES...

PERHAPS...

WHY ARE WE STOPPING?

IT'S HIM!

WHAT ARE YOU WAITING FOR, LACKEY?

HOT OR COLD, RAIN DOESN'T MAKE ANY DIFFERENCE TO ME...

BLOW BLOW BLOW BLOW BLOW

47

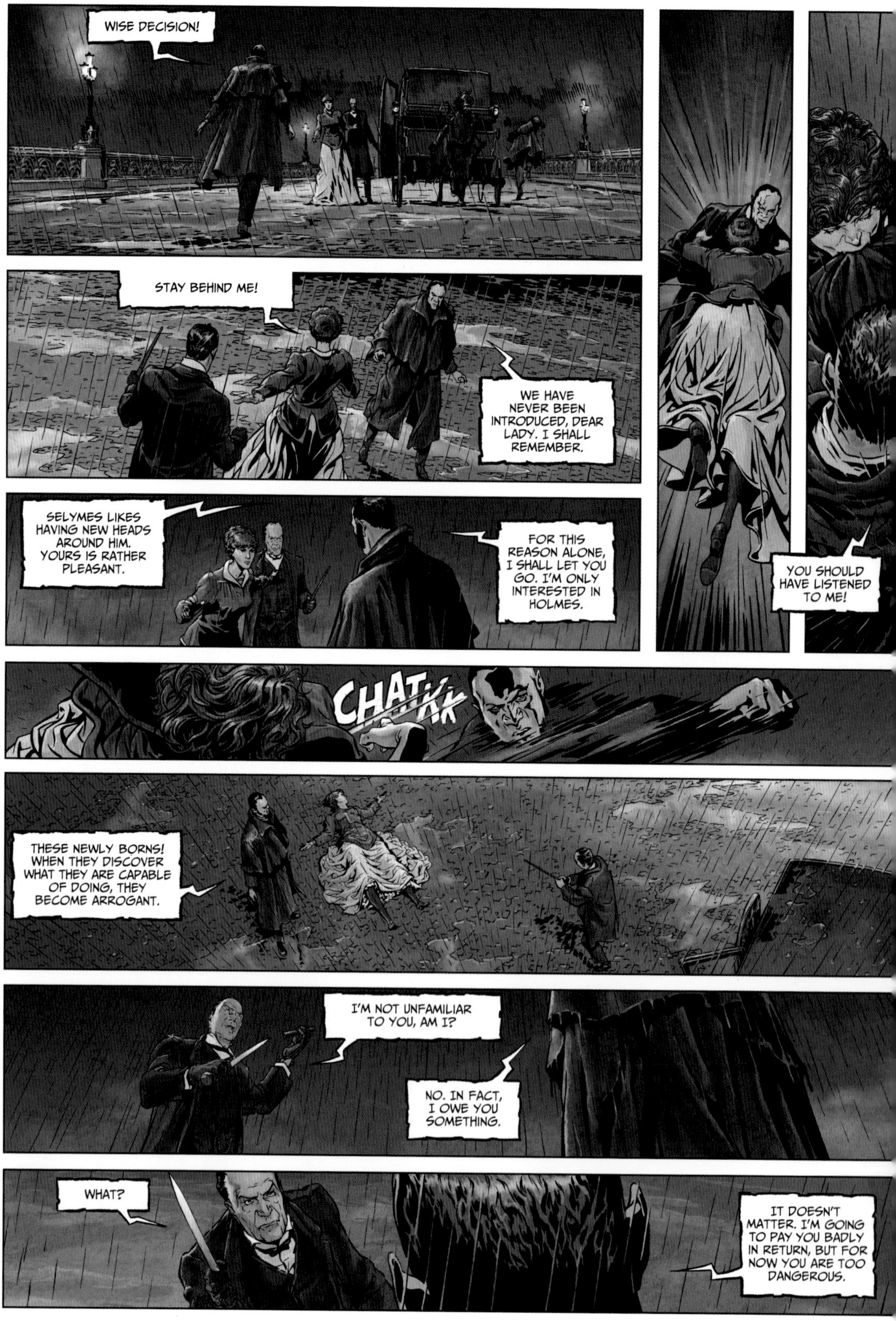
WISE DECISION!
STAY BEHIND ME!
WE HAVE NEVER BEEN INTRODUCED, DEAR LADY. I SHALL REMEMBER.
SELYMES LIKES HAVING NEW HEADS AROUND HIM. YOURS IS RATHER PLEASANT.
FOR THIS REASON ALONE, I SHALL LET YOU GO. I'M ONLY INTERESTED IN HOLMES.
YOU SHOULD HAVE LISTENED TO ME!
CHATKK
THESE NEWLY BORNS! WHEN THEY DISCOVER WHAT THEY ARE CAPABLE OF DOING, THEY BECOME ARROGANT.
I'M NOT UNFAMILIAR TO YOU, AM I?
NO. IN FACT, I OWE YOU SOMETHING.
WHAT?
IT DOESN'T MATTER. I'M GOING TO PAY YOU BADLY IN RETURN, BUT FOR NOW YOU ARE TOO DANGEROUS.

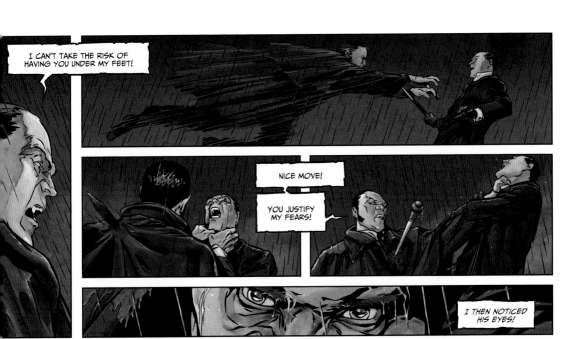

I CAN'T TAKE THE RISK OF HAVING YOU UNDER MY FEET!

NICE MOVE!

YOU JUSTIFY MY FEARS!

I THEN NOTICED HIS EYES!

IT'S TIME TO SAY GOODBYE, HOLMES!

FOR SOMEONE WHO DOESN'T BELIEVE IN THE FORCE OF DESTINY, I MUST ADMIT THAT FATE WAS CURIOUSLY IN MY FAVOR.

KRAKOOM

SHHHH

I KNEW THAT MY ADVANTAGE WOULDN'T LAST LONG.

THAT I HAD TO SEIZE MY CHANCE.

BUT CHANES WAS NOTHING LIKE A CONSENTING VICTIM. AND WHAT STRENGTH!

THE FALL SEEMED TO LAST AN ETERNITY.

UNTIL I FELT COLD ENTER ME...

...AND CHASE THE AIR FROM MY LUNGS.

AN ICY NIGHT ENVELOPED ME LITTLE BY LITTLE.

I LOST CONSCIOUSNESS.

ONE WAY OR ANOTHER, THEY ARE ALL AWARE. THEY KNOW THAT ADVERSITY WILL COME SOONER OR LATER TO INJURE THEIR LIVES.

HAPPINESS IS FRAGILE, DESTRUCTIBLE... BUT THIS IS A REALITY THEY CAN DEAL WITH.

THEY CARRY ON, SAVORING EACH MOMENT, EACH LOVED ONE.

I OFTEN WONDER... IF I HADN'T SPENT SO MANY YEARS STUDYING THE BLACKNESS OF THE HUMAN SOUL, WOULD I HAVE FOLLOWED THAT PATH?

"THORNY QUESTION!" WOULD YOU REPLY, WATSON, BECAUSE THE ANSWER IS OBVIOUS.

I'M NOT A MAN TO BE GOVERNED BY SENTIMENTS. EVEN IF I WANTED TO, IT'S TOO LATE TO CHANGE.

IF I WANT TO FINISH THE TALE I'VE PROMISED YOU BEFORE NIGHT FALLS, I MUST GO BACK TO THE HOTEL.

MY LAST BLUE SKY.

LONDON, 22ND
JUNE 1891.

HNNGHH...

CONSIDER YOURSELF
LUCKY. YOU SHOULD BE AT
THE BOTTOM OF THE RIVER.
I DIVED IN WITHOUT MUCH
HOPE OF SAVING YOU.

CHANES...

NO TRACE. THE
CURRENT MUST
HAVE TAKEN HIM
FURTHER DOWN.

HE... WAS SEVERELY
WOUNDED.

HIS WOUNDS DON'T MATTER. IF HE DIDN'T DIE BEFORE YOUR EYES, CONSIDER THAT HE WILL RECOVER.

AND AS THE THAMES'S MUDDY WATERS DIDN'T CLAIM HIM, WE ARE BACK TO THE START.

NOT QUITE.

FOR A REASON THAT ESCAPES ME, CHANES HAS SET THIS TRAP FOR US. HE WANTED ME DEAD, AND I'M STILL HERE. IT'S A SMALL VICTORY...

SELYMES WILL VIEW THAT DIFFERENTLY. CHANES UNMASKED HIMSELF. WE NEARLY CAUGHT HIM... EVEN IF I FEAR HIS JUDGMENT, I MUST INFORM MY MASTER OF OUR FAILURE.

HE WILL WAIT, MRS. MIDDLES. COME WITH ME BACK TO THE LABORATORY.

WHY SHOULD I DO THAT?

SO YOU WON'T HAVE ONLY BAD NEWS WHEN YOU SEE HIM. MY DUEL WITH CHANES WAS FULL OF INFORMATION.

I PERHAPS HAVE A LEAD. I SHALL ONLY BE SURE WHEN I'VE DONE SOME MANIPULATIONS. WOULD YOU REALLY PREFER TO CONFRONT SELYMES AT ONCE? I DON'T THINK SO...

TAKE YOUR HAND AWAY.

GOOD GOD! YOU'RE SAFE! WE HEARD THE SHOTS BUT THE TIME TO--

ENOUGH, MR. CARDY.

IF YOU WANT TO BE USEFUL, ESCORT US BACK TO THE CARRIAGE. WE ARE IN A HURRY!

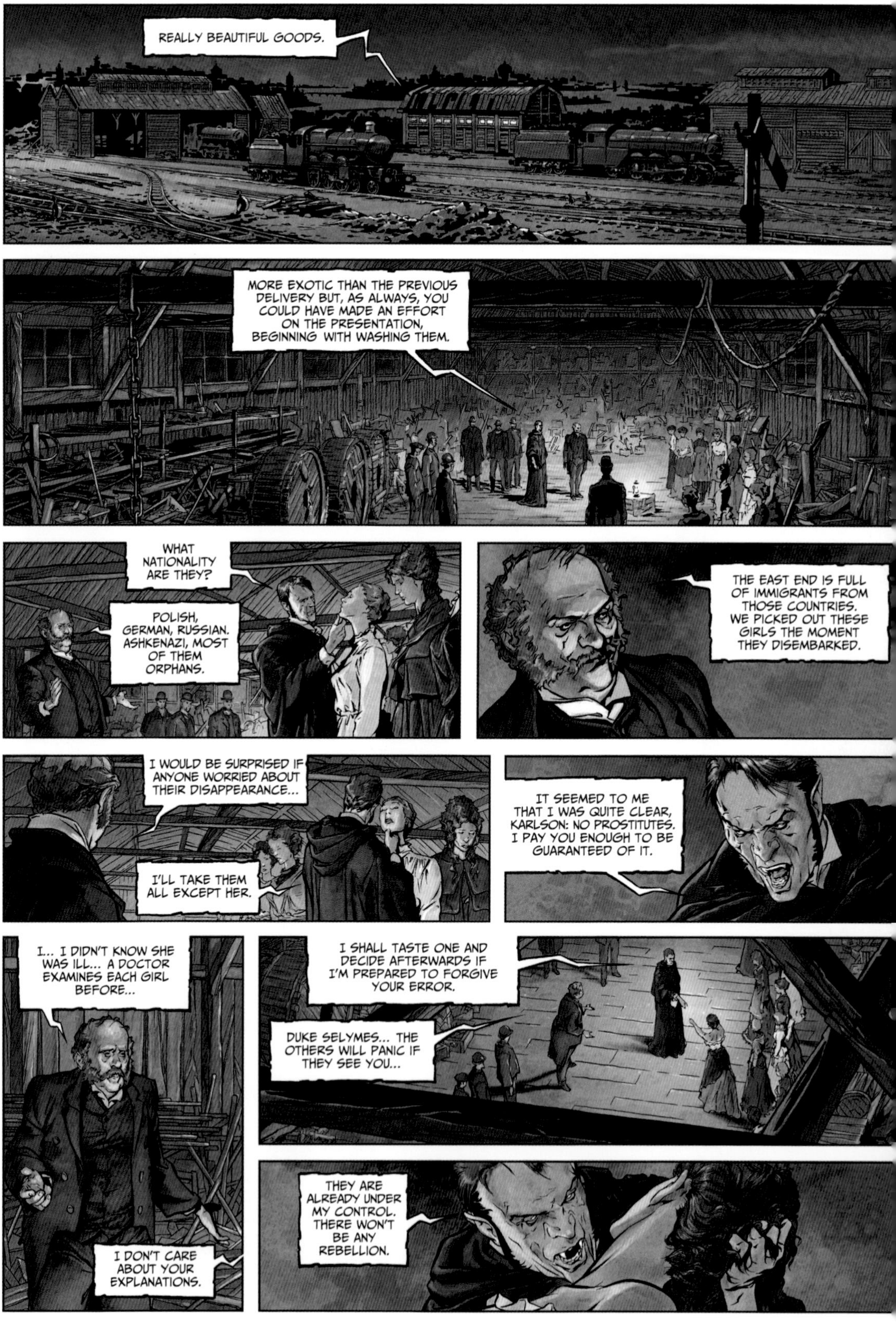
REALLY BEAUTIFUL GOODS.
MORE EXOTIC THAN THE PREVIOUS DELIVERY BUT, AS ALWAYS, YOU COULD HAVE MADE AN EFFORT ON THE PRESENTATION, BEGINNING WITH WASHING THEM.
WHAT NATIONALITY ARE THEY?
POLISH, GERMAN, RUSSIAN. ASHKENAZI, MOST OF THEM ORPHANS.
THE EAST END IS FULL OF IMMIGRANTS FROM THOSE COUNTRIES. WE PICKED OUT THESE GIRLS THE MOMENT THEY DISEMBARKED.
I WOULD BE SURPRISED IF ANYONE WORRIED ABOUT THEIR DISAPPEARANCE...
I'LL TAKE THEM ALL EXCEPT HER.
IT SEEMED TO ME THAT I WAS QUITE CLEAR, KARLSON: NO PROSTITUTES. I PAY YOU ENOUGH TO BE GUARANTEED OF IT.
I... I DIDN'T KNOW SHE WAS ILL... A DOCTOR EXAMINES EACH GIRL BEFORE...
I DON'T CARE ABOUT YOUR EXPLANATIONS.
I SHALL TASTE ONE AND DECIDE AFTERWARDS IF I'M PREPARED TO FORGIVE YOUR ERROR.
DUKE SELYMES... THE OTHERS WILL PANIC IF THEY SEE YOU...
THEY ARE ALREADY UNDER MY CONTROL. THERE WON'T BE ANY REBELLION.

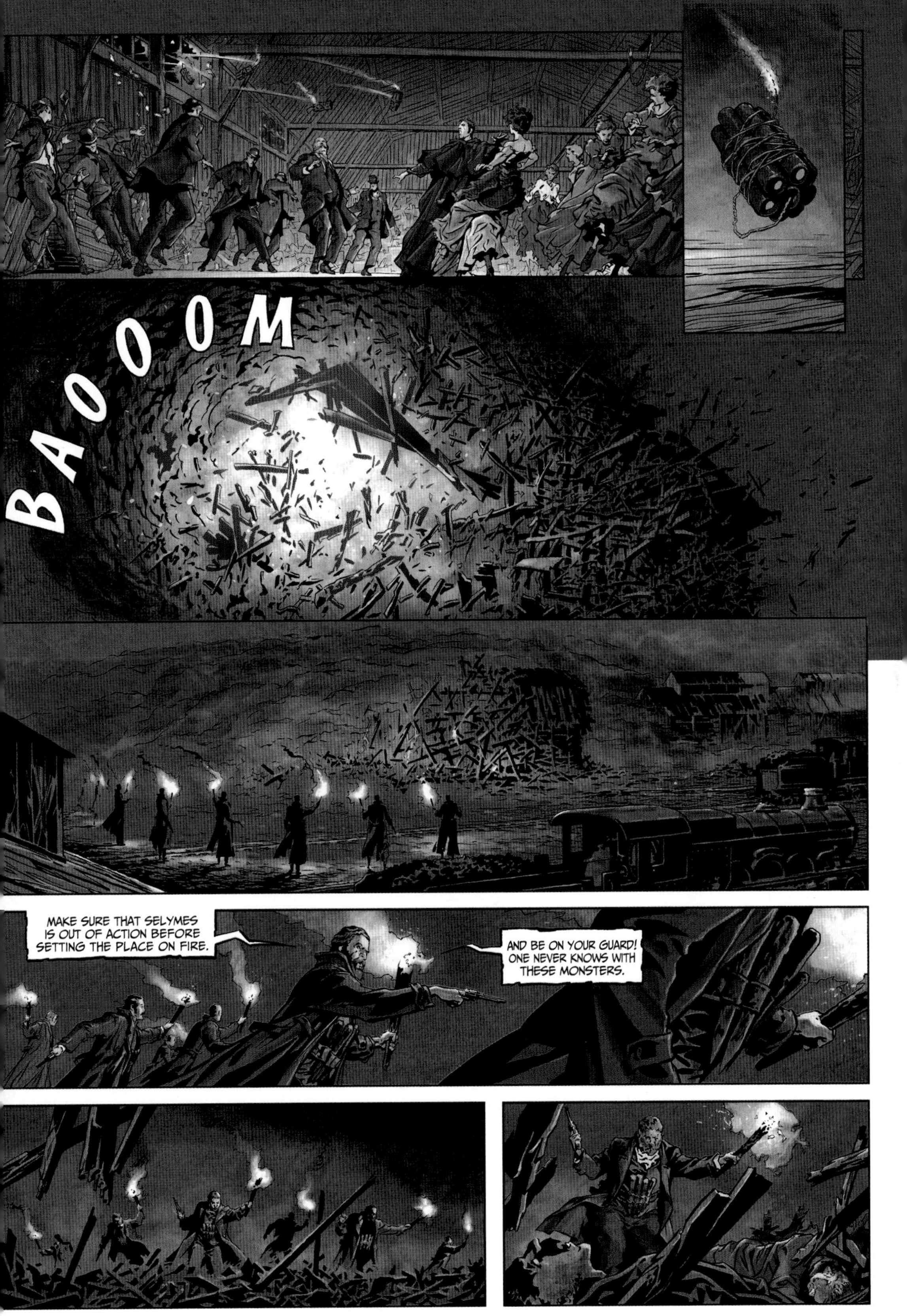
BAOOOM
MAKE SURE THAT SELYMES IS OUT OF ACTION BEFORE SETTING THE PLACE ON FIRE.
AND BE ON YOUR GUARD! ONE NEVER KNOWS WITH THESE MONSTERS.

THIS ONE IS STILL BREATHING!

BLAMM

IT WAS A YOUNG GIRL.

YOU KNOW WHAT WAS AWAITING HER. BETTER SHE LEFT THAT WAY.

I'VE A VAMPIRE HERE!

DIDN'T THINK I'D HAVE THE CHANCE TO GET ONE.

BEFORE FINISHING OFF MY PEOPLE...

...SAVE YOUR OWN LIVES!

SLASHHH

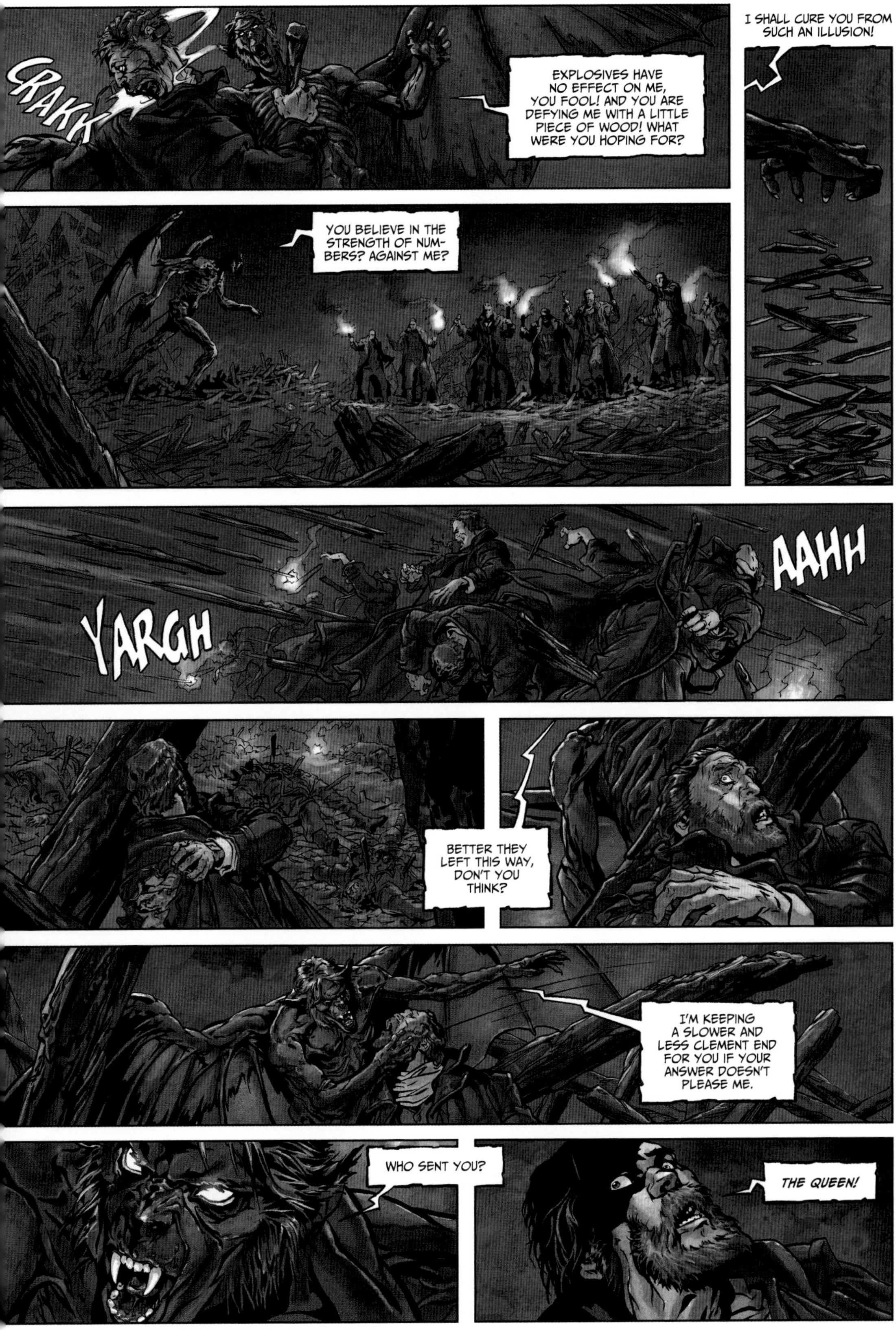
CRAKK
EXPLOSIVES HAVE NO EFFECT ON ME, YOU FOOL! AND YOU ARE DEFYING ME WITH A LITTLE PIECE OF WOOD! WHAT WERE YOU HOPING FOR?
YOU BELIEVE IN THE STRENGTH OF NUMBERS? AGAINST ME?
I SHALL CURE YOU FROM SUCH AN ILLUSION!
YARGH
AAHH
BETTER THEY LEFT THIS WAY, DON'T YOU THINK?
I'M KEEPING A SLOWER AND LESS CLEMENT END FOR YOU IF YOUR ANSWER DOESN'T PLEASE ME.
WHO SENT YOU?
THE QUEEN!

WITH REGARD TO DRUGS, I CONSIDER MYSELF, WITHOUT PRETENSION, AS AN EXPERT. I'VE TRIED THEM ALL, OR ALMOST.

FOR EXAMPLE, AN ABNORMAL DILATION OF THE PUPILS IS AN INTERESTING INDICATION.

I CAN DESCRIBE THEIR EFFECTS AND DETERMINE THE NATURE OF A SUBSTANCE BY THE SYMPTOMS THAT THE USER SHOWS.

BUT NOT SUFFICIENT TO DRAW FINAL CONCLUSIONS. THAT'S WHERE MY TALENT FOR CHEMISTRY COMES IN.

YOU KNOW BETTER THAN ANYBODY, WATSON, THAT IF THERE IS A FIELD IN WHICH I EXCEL, IT'S THAT ONE. THE HARDEST WORK WAS TO FIND THE MEANS TO MAKE CHANES'S BLOOD COAGULATE.

I MANAGED TO DO SO, NOT WITHOUT DIFFICULTY. THE REST WAS EASY.

I DON'T KNOW HOW LONG THE PROCESSES TOOK. I DID SEVERAL AT THE SAME TIME...

THE MAIN THING IS THAT ONE OF THEM GAVE ME THE ANSWER I WAS LOOKING FOR.

MORPHINE ACETATE!

THE INORDINATE PROPORTIONS HE WAS TAKING COULD WIPE OUT AN ENTIRE VILLAGE.

CHANES DIDN'T HAVE TO
WORRY ABOUT THE PRO-
DUCT'S DANGER. A POISON
CAN'T KILL A CREATURE THAT
DOESN'T BELONG TO THE
WORLD OF THE LIVING.

HIS CONSUMPTION MADE
OF HIM AN ATYPICAL CLIENT.
ENOUGH TO AWAKEN THE
CURIOSITY OF HIS SUPPLIER.

IT WOULDN'T
TAKE ME LONG
TO FIND OUT WHO
SUPPLIED HIM.

I WAS SO ABSORBED
BY MY PROGRESS
THAT I DIDN'T SEE
THE STORM COMING.

DON'T YOU
HAVE SOMETHING
TO SAY TO ME,
JOYCE?

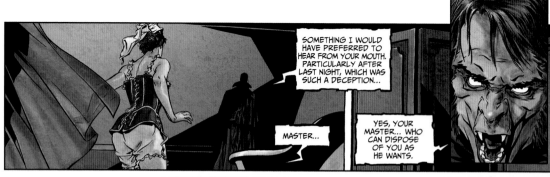

SOMETHING I WOULD HAVE PREFERRED TO HEAR FROM YOUR MOUTH. PARTICULARLY AFTER LAST NIGHT, WHICH WAS SUCH A DECEPTION...

MASTER...

YES, YOUR MASTER... WHO CAN DISPOSE OF YOU AS HE WANTS.

BLOOMM

?!

WHAT THE...?!

KRAKK

KLING KLAC

AAHHH!!

THE UNACCEPTABLE IS THAT CHANES IS STILL IN THIS WORLD!

I DON'T DENY IT! BUT GIVE ME SOME TIME! I KNOW HOW TO FIND HIM! EVERYTHING IS NOT LOST!

THIS IS UNACCEPTABLE! YOU CAN'T EXPECT THE IMPOSSIBLE FROM ME AND DESTROY MY WORK IN A FIT OF TEMPER!

THAT DEPENDS FOR WHOM, HOLMES. I HAVE ALREADY WARNED YOU SUFFICIENTLY.

FOLLOW ME OR MY SERVANTS WILL DRAG YOU.

LATER. EARL'S COURT ROAD.

THAT'S A VERY UGLY HOME. I SUPPOSE THAT IT'S A QUESTION OF TASTE.

THIS IS NOT NECESSARY!

IT'S ONLY A QUESTION OF HOURS, AT THE MOST ONE OR TWO DAYS, BEFORE CHANES IS HANDED OVER TO YOU!

I BELIEVE THAT YOU ARE SINCERE, AS I WAS DURING OUR LAST MEETING...

HAVE NO FEAR FOR THE LIFE OF YOUR FRIEND WATSON. I SHAN'T HURT HIM... AT LEAST NOT FOR THE TIME BEING.

BUT I WON'T GIVE THE SAME PROMISE WITH REGARD TO HIS DELIGHTFUL WIFE...

SELYMES!

CALM DOWN! YOU WILL ATTRACT ATTENTION TO US AND YOU WOULDN'T LIKE THE CONSEQUENCES.

LOOK, HOLMES! WATCH LIKE NO MAN BEFORE!

BESIDES, WE HAVE AN EXPERIENCE TO SHARE.

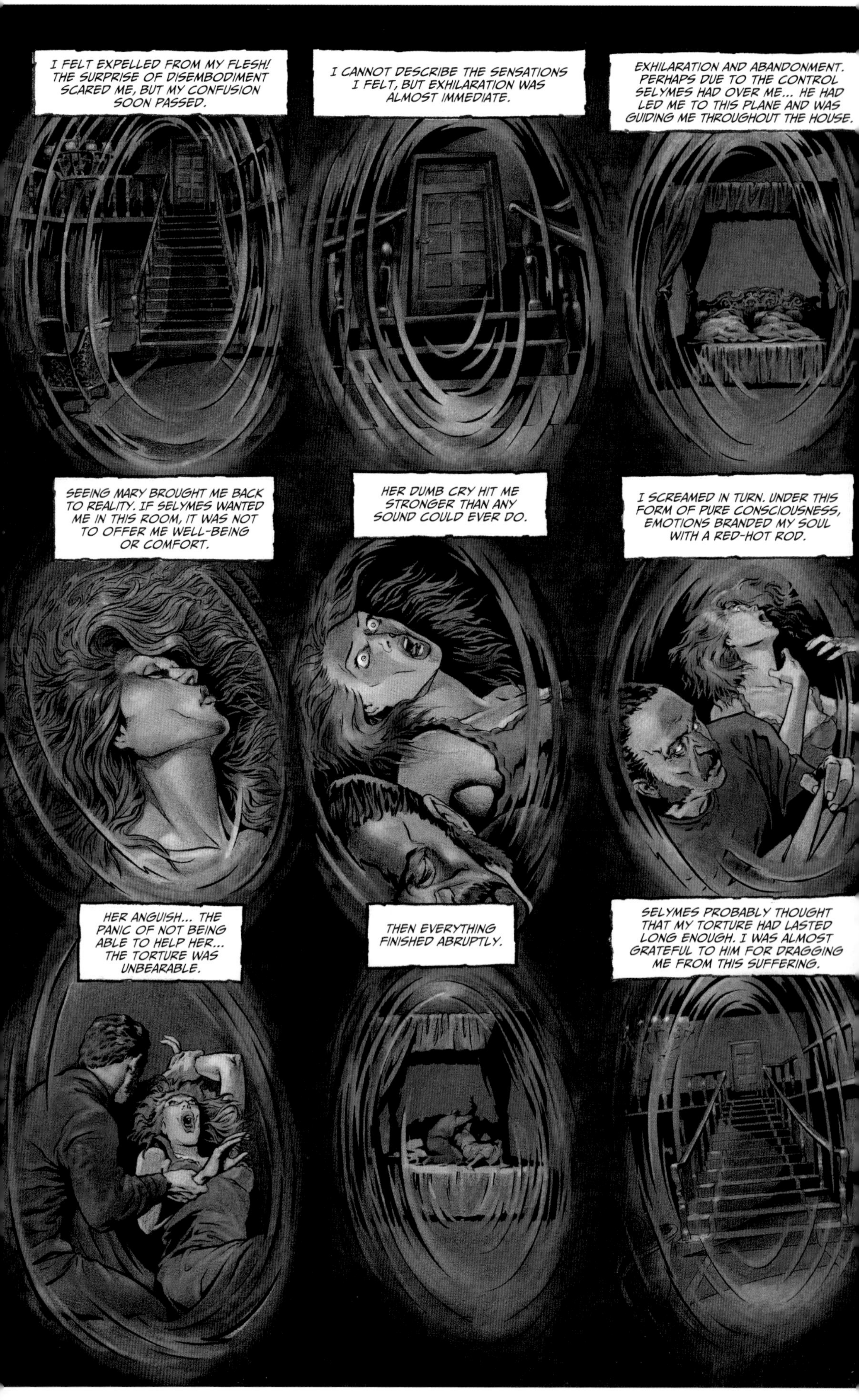

I FELT EXPELLED FROM MY FLESH! THE SURPRISE OF DISEMBODIMENT SCARED ME, BUT MY CONFUSION SOON PASSED.
I CANNOT DESCRIBE THE SENSATIONS I FELT, BUT EXHILARATION WAS ALMOST IMMEDIATE.
EXHILARATION AND ABANDONMENT. PERHAPS DUE TO THE CONTROL SELYMES HAD OVER ME... HE HAD LED ME TO THIS PLANE AND WAS GUIDING ME THROUGHOUT THE HOUSE.
SEEING MARY BROUGHT ME BACK TO REALITY. IF SELYMES WANTED ME IN THIS ROOM, IT WAS NOT TO OFFER ME WELL-BEING OR COMFORT.
HER DUMB CRY HIT ME STRONGER THAN ANY SOUND COULD EVER DO.
I SCREAMED IN TURN. UNDER THIS FORM OF PURE CONSCIOUSNESS, EMOTIONS BRANDED MY SOUL WITH A RED-HOT ROD.
HER ANGUISH... THE PANIC OF NOT BEING ABLE TO HELP HER... THE TORTURE WAS UNBEARABLE.
THEN EVERYTHING FINISHED ABRUPTLY.
SELYMES PROBABLY THOUGHT THAT MY TORTURE HAD LASTED LONG ENOUGH. I WAS ALMOST GRATEFUL TO HIM FOR DRAGGING ME FROM THIS SUFFERING.

AAHHHH!

MARY...

BE ASSURED, SHE WILL LIVE. BUT THIS EXPERIENCE WILL LEAVE DEEP SCARS FROM WHICH SHE WILL NEVER REALLY RECOVER.

DID YOU FEEL HER SUFFERING? AS FOR ME, I HAVE LOST NOTHING OF IT.

WHEN DEATH APPROACHES, THE MIND GENERATES REAL MENTAL IMAGES...

YOU BLOODY--

SHOULD WE KEEP HIM, MASTER?

DON'T STOOP TO INSULT ME. THAT WILL SOLVE NOTHING.

NO. LET HIM GET OVER THE SHOCK. HE WILL SOON COME BACK TO ME.

I KNOW THAT HE WILL GIVE THE BEST OF HIMSELF FROM NOW ON.

MY DEAR WATSON, WILL YOU FORGIVE ME IF I TELL YOU THAT I HAVE NEVER ACTED SO WELL UP TO NOW?

I DIDN'T UNDERESTIMATE THE DRAMA THAT WAS YOURS. BUT SELYMES HAD TO BELIEVE THAT I WAS UNDER HIS CONTROL. VULNERABLE. I KNEW THAT HE WOULD THUS LEAVE ME MORE SPACE TO ACT.

BY ATTACKING MARY AND YOU, HE HAD COMMITTED HIS GRAVEST MISTAKE.

IT TOOK ME TWO GOOD HOURS TO GET TO BAKER STREET.

FOR MANY REASONS, I COULDN'T GO IN THROUGH THE FRONT DOOR. THE FIRST REASON OF ALL WAS THAT MORIARTY'S MEN WERE WATCHING MY HOME.

IT WAS THEREFORE BETTER TO OPT TO BREAK IN, WITH THE NONNEGLIGIBLE ADVANTAGE THAT THE SASH WINDOW WAS EASY TO FORCE. I KNEW THAT ONE DAY OR ANOTHER, SUCH AN ACCESS WOULD BE OF USE TO ME.

I WASN'T SURPRISED TO SEE THAT MRS. HUDSON HAD NOT TOUCHED MY EFFECTS.

FOLLOWING A MISSION I HAD UNDERTAKEN FOR THE DUTCH ROYAL FAMILY, I HAD RECEIVED A SUM OF MONEY THAT WAS ALMOST INDECENT. I USED IT TO PAY MY LANDLADY SEVERAL YEARS' RENT IN ADVANCE. EVEN IF THIS CHOICE SEEMS STRANGE TO YOU, YOU MUST UNDERSTAND THAT I HAD ABSOLUTE COMFORT WITHIN THESE WALLS.

MRS. HUDSON WAS VERY SERIOUS ABOUT COMMITMENTS. THE FACT THAT I HAD BEEN DECLARED DEAD DIDN'T SEEM TO COME INTO IT.

DAY WAS SOON TO BREAK. I HAD TO HURRY...

...OTHERWISE THIS DEAR WOMAN WOULD SURPRISE ME AND HER HEART WOULD NOT HOLD OUT.

Shadwell's Butcher

THE FACTS THAT INTERESTED ME DATED BACK TO 1876. THAT WAS BEFORE I CREATED THE PROFESSION OF AN ADVISORY PRIVATE DETECTIVE.

I HAD PUT AN END TO THE SERIES OF MURDERS COMMITTED BY BRUCE BURBON, WHOM THE PRESS HAD NICKNAMED THE BUTCHER OF SHADWELL.

HE SEQUESTERED HIS VICTIMS AND TORTURED THEM TO DEATH. SAMANTHA AND PERRY CHANES, HIS LAST PREY, DIED JUST BEFORE I CAUGHT HIM.

THE COUPLE LEFT TWO CHILDREN, WHO WERE HANDED OVER TO THE CHILD WELFARE SERVICE. ONE WAS CALLED SIMON...

...THE OTHER, OWEN.

SO, THAT WAS WHAT CHANES WAS TALKING ABOUT. I HAD SAVED HIM AND HIS BROTHER... AND I HAD AVENGED THE DEATH OF THEIR PARENTS.

OWEN WAS ABOUT 16 OR 17 AT THE TIME. TO SEE HIS PARENTS MURDERED WHEN SO YOUNG FORMS A PERSON.

BUT THAT DOES NOT EXCUSE HIS CURRENT ACTS.

I PRETENDED TO VISIT AGAIN ALL THE INFORMERS. PRETENDED BECAUSE, THIS TIME, I KNEW WHO TO TURN TO.

AS I HAD FORESEEN, AS THE VISITS WENT ON, MY CHAPERONES BECAME LESS AND LESS WATCHFUL. I TOOK THEM FOR A WALK FOR HALF A DAY BEFORE GOING TO SEE NORTON FISBACK.

IN HIS FORMER LIFE, FISBACK HAD BEEN A PETTY THUG. HIS GANG HAD HAD PROBLEMS WITH MORIARTY, AND ONLY HE REMAINED TO GIVE EVIDENCE.

I HAD HELPED HIM TO CHANGE HIS LIFE BEFORE HE SHARED THE LOT OF HIS ACOLYTES. HE HAD OPENED A BARREL-MAKING FIRM, AND BUSINESS WAS FLOURISHING.

MR. FISBACK, COULD YOU SPARE ME A MOMENT, PLEASE?

FISBACK HAD BEEN AN EXCELLENT PICKPOCKET, WHICH WAS A DISCIPLINE REQUIRING A KEEN SENSE OF OBSERVATION.

MR. FISBACK?

EXCUSE ME...

AFTER YOU...

THEY SAID YOU WERE DEAD...

PRETEND I AM...

WHICH DETAIL BETRAYED ME?

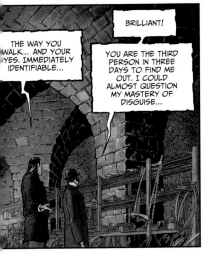

THE WAY YOU WALK... AND YOUR EYES. IMMEDIATELY IDENTIFIABLE...

BRILLIANT!

YOU ARE THE THIRD PERSON IN THREE DAYS TO FIND ME OUT. I COULD ALMOST QUESTION MY MASTERY OF DISGUISE...

YOU HAVE CERTAINLY SEEN THE CHAPS STICKING TO MY HEELS.

HARD NOT TO SEE THEM. IF YOU'D LIKE ME TO GET RID OF THEM, I CAN--

THANK YOU. BUT I DIDN'T COME ABOUT THAT. I AM ENQUIRING ABOUT A MAN WHO BUYS LARGE QUANTITIES OF MORPHINE ACETATE.

I WOULD LIKE TO KNOW WHO PROCURES IT FOR HIM WITHOUT ALERTING MY... COMPANIONS.

I KNOW THAT YOU HAVE KEPT FRIENDLY WITH THE OPIUM MERCHANTS. WOULD YOU AGREE TO GIVING ME INFORMATION?

I COULDN'T REFUSE YOU ANYTHING BEFORE YOU DEALT WITH THAT BASTARD MORIARTY, SO NOW...

ARE YOU SURE THAT HE'S DEAD?

NO DOUBT. I SAW HIM CRASH ON THE ROCKS. NO ONE COULD SURVIVE SUCH A FALL.

WHAT DOES YOUR BUYER LOOK LIKE?

SHE WILL GIVE YOU A BRIEF INTERVIEW.

YOU ARE TOO PROUD TO SHOW IT, BUT I KNOW THIS PLACE MAKES YOU UNEASY.

AS MUCH AS CHANES'S CRIMES ANNOY ME, I HOPE.

I UNDERSTAND YOUR IMPATIENCE, YOUR MAJESTY, BUT IN THE NAME OF THE SACRED LINKS THAT UNITE OUR FAMILIES, GIVE ME THE TIME TO RESOLVE THIS BUSINESS.

I DON'T WANT TO OPPOSE YOU...

DO YOU REALLY THINK THAT LAST NIGHT'S ATTACK WAS AIMED AT GETTING RID OF YOU?

I WOULD NOT HAVE SENT OUT SUCH AN ILL-PREPARED COMMANDO IF I HAD WISHED TO DO SO.

AS FOR THE VEILED THREAT, WE BOTH KNOW THAT YOU CANNOT HARM ME. MY PLACE IN HISTORY HAS ALREADY BEEN WRITTEN.

WHEREAS THE FLAME OF YOUR SPECIES CAN BE EXTINGUISHED AT ANY MOMENT.

SO THAT YOU CAN HEAR THIS FOR YOURSELF: CHANE'S VENDETTA MUST STOP IMMEDIATELY. IF YOU DON'T BRING ME HIS ASHES SOON, OR IF HE ATTACKS ANOTHER PERSON CLOSE TO ME...

IF I HAD TO CHOOSE, I WOULD PREFER TO HAVE YOU WITH ME, SELYMES. BUT THAT ONLY DEPENDS ON YOU. THE LINKS YOU TALKED ABOUT... THAT'S WHY I ACCEPTED TO RECEIVE YOU.

...THIS MEETING WILL BE OUR FAREWELL.

69

WHAT A STINK!

THIS IS THE SEVENTH SO-CALLED HIDING PLACE THAT WE HAVE VISITED. YOUR INFORMERS ARE TAKING US FOR A RIDE.

THE ONLY DEAD CREATURE HERE IS THIS DOG.

AN ENQUIRY IS NOT SOLVED BY ITSELF. THIS TRACK IS PERHAPS A DEAD END... OR PERHAPS IT WILL HELP US TO FIND CHANES.

LET'S SEARCH THE CELLAR AND IF THERE REALLY IS NOTHING THERE...

AS YOU WISH.

BUT IT'S A WASTE OF TIME. IN SPITE OF THE STINK, I WOULD KNOW IF HE HAD STAYED IN THIS RUBBISH HEAP.

I WOULD SMELL HIS—

SHE WASN'T WARY OF ME. THAT HELPED, UNDOUBTEDLY...

...BUT NOT AS MUCH AS THE STINK COMING FROM THE DEAD DOG. IT COVERED THE SMELL OF ETHER LONG ENOUGH FOR ME TO SURPRISE HER.

IF DRUGS WORKED ON VAMPIRES, CHLOROFORM SHOULD HAVE ITS EFFECT.

SHE WAS STRONG. BUT NOT ENOUGH TO FREE HERSELF FROM THE ARMLOCK. I WAS NONETHELESS PLEASED TO SEE HER LET GO.

I DIDN'T HOPE TO KEEP HER INDEFINITELY. JUST A FEW HOURS... UNTIL DAWN.

AFTERWARDS, THE SUN WOULD TAKE OVER.

SELYMES DECIDEDLY HAD WELL UNDERSTOOD ME.

THINKING ABOUT IT AGAIN, I HAD NEVER AT ANY TIME ENVISAGED KILLING HER. I COULD HAVE USED ANOTHER MESSENGER...

THE NEXT TIME YOU NEED A DEAD DOG, YOU CAN GO THERE YOURSELF. THE STINK IS STILL STICKING TO MY SKIN.

BELIEVE IN MY GRATITUDE, FISBACK. IT WILL BE EVEN GREATER IF YOU KNOW WHO SUPPLIES CHANES.

IT'S LI WANG. I'M GIVEN TO BELIEVE THAT CHANES FRIGHTENS HIM BUT AS HE PAYS IMMEDIATELY, THE CHINK MAKES AN EFFORT.

HE DELIVERS HIM EVERY EVENING THE ACETATE HE HAS MANAGED TO COLLECT. IF YOUR CHAP DOESN'T CALM DOWN, HE WON'T LIVE LONG.

HE WOULD SURPRISE YOU.

YOU HAVE NO IDEA OF THE SERVICE YOU ARE RENDERING ME.

YOU ARE STILL IN ADVANCE OF SERVICES RENDERED. SOMETHING TELLS ME THAT I WON'T SEE YOU AGAIN SOON, NO?

WHO KNOWS WHAT WILL HAPPEN TOMORROW?

I HAD NEVER HAD ANY BUSINESS WITH LI WANG, BUT HE WASN'T UNKNOWN TO ME.

HE HAD BEEN ONE OF THE FIRST TO IMPORT AND TRADE OPIUM IN LONDON. I WAITED FOR HIM AT THE DOOR OF HIS OPIUM DEN, LOCATED AT THE HEART OF WHITECHAPEL.

I ONLY HAD TO FOLLOW HIM. HE DIDN'T CHECK ONCE IF HE WAS BEING FOLLOWED. CHANES PROBABLY OBSESSED HIM...

FOR SUCH AN IMPORTANT CLIENT, IT WAS OBVIOUS THAT WANG WOULD TAKE THE ACETATE HIMSELF. IT WOULD MAKE THE TASK EASIER FOR ME.

MY PREY WAS HIDING AT STEPNEY, IN THE WORST PART OF THE DISTRICT. A PLACE WHERE EVEN A VAMPIRE WOULD FEEL IN DANGER.

WANG HANDED OVER THE GOODS, THEN LEFT RAPIDLY.

I WAS CONVINCED THAT AT SUCH A LEVEL OF DEPENDENCY, CHANES WOULD SWALLOW ALL OR PART OF THE DRUG... AT LEAST A FISTFUL OF SEEDS.

ON HIM, THE POISON HAD, AT THE WORST, A NARCOTIC AND RELAXING EFFECT.

AFTER WAITING FOR AN HOUR, I WENT INTO HIS LAIR...

?!

HOLMES...

YOUR... TIMING IS PERFECT. I WON'T RESIST YOU... VERY MUCH.

I DIDN'T COME TO FIGHT. BUT I'M GLAD TO SEE YOU IN THIS STATE. WE CAN TALK WITHOUT YOU JUMPING AT MY THROAT.

I KNOW WHO YOU ARE, AND I CAN IMAGINE WHAT YOU HAVE SUFFERED...

CAN YOU?

"THE MURDER OF MY PARENTS WAS ONLY A START... AFTER TIME SPENT AT THE ORPHANAGE, SIMON AND I WERE SEPARATED.

"AS I COULDN'T STAND LOSING HIM, I FLED FROM MY FOSTER FAMILY AND LOOKED FOR HIM. IN VAIN...

"I WAS UNDER THE LAW OF THE STREET FOR SOME YEARS. WHEN I WAS 25, I WAS CALLED 'WITHOUT HEART.' I WAS FEARED THROUGHOUT THE EAST END...

"IT WAS THEN THAT SELYMES NOTICED ME. SOMETHING IN ME FASCINATED HIM. HE WANTED ME BY HIS SIDE, AND TOOK CARE OF MY TRANSFORMATION."

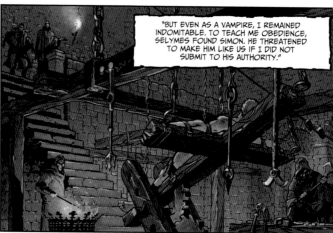

"BUT EVEN AS A VAMPIRE, I REMAINED INDOMITABLE. TO TEACH ME OBEDIENCE, SELYMES FOUND SIMON. HE THREATENED TO MAKE HIM LIKE US IF I DID NOT SUBMIT TO HIS AUTHORITY."

I WAS GOING TO YIELD WHEN THE SICKNESS DECLARED ITSELF...

SELYMES HAS TOLD ME OF THE RAGE THAT SEIZES YOU.

HE HAS CERTAIN[LY] FORGOTTEN T[O] TELL YOU THE ORIGIN OF THE SICKNESS. SELYM[ES] TRANSMITTED IT [TO] ME BY DRINKIN[G] MY BLOOD.

"HE CONTAMINATED ME, JUST AS HE HAD INFECTED MANY OTHERS BEFORE ME. I INCARNATED HIS SHAME, THE PROOF OF HIS IMPURITY. WHEN MY MADNESS WAS DECLARED, HE TRIED TO GET RID OF ME.

"AT THE END OF HIS PATIENCE, THE VAMPIRE MASTER DECIDED TO PUSH ME TO MY LIMITS. HE TORTURED SIMON AND TORE OUT HIS HEART AS AN ECHO TO MY NICKNAME.

"AS HIS MESSENGERS SUCCUMBED ONE AFTER THE OTHER, HE USED SIMON TO BRING ME BACK TO HIM. BUT TO HELP MY BROTHER WOULD BE TO CONDEMN BOTH OF US. SELYMES WOULD NEVER HAVE LET HIM GO.

"SELYMES'S STRATEGY PAID. I WAS LOCKED IN A DUNGEON, WHERE MY BROTHER'S BODY KEPT ME COMPANY.

"FOR THREE YEARS, MY HATRED GREW DEEPER. THEN I FINALLY ESCAPED FROM MY JAILERS..."

...TO START A SERIES OF BARBARIC CRIMES. SO BESTIAL THAT--

BESTIAL? PERHAPS. SYMBOLIC, SURELY.

SHORTLY AFTER LEAVING THE DUNGEON, I STARTED TO USE DRUGS. NOT TO FALL INTO DEBAUCHERY BUT WITH THE HOPE THAT THE OPIATES WOULD HELP ME CONTROL MY FITS OF MADNESS.

NOTHING WORKED UNTIL I USED MORPHINE ACETATE.

SO YOU DIDN'T COMMIT THESE MURDERS OUT OF INSTINCT BUT IN COLD BLOOD... THE ACT IS EVEN MORE CRIMINAL.

ACETATE IS NOT EFFICIENT TO THAT POINT. AND AFTER THREE YEARS OF WATCHING RATS NIBBLE AT SIMON'S BODY, I BECAME EVEN WILDER THAN BEFORE. THIS BEING SAID, MY VICTIMS WERE NOT CHOSEN BY CHANCE.

LORD BATTENKEY HAD BEATEN HIS ONLY SON TO DEATH. THE PROSTITUTE I KILLED BLACKMAILED HER REGULAR CLIENTS. SOMERSETT HAD ARRANGED THE SUICIDE OF A MALE LOVER WHO WAS TOO LOQUACIOUS ABOUT THEIR SEXUAL BEHAVIOR. I COULD CONTINUE THE LIST...

AND THE CLUB MEMBERS?

LI WANG DIDN'T DELIVER TO ME THAT DAY. I COULDN'T CONTROL MYSELF...

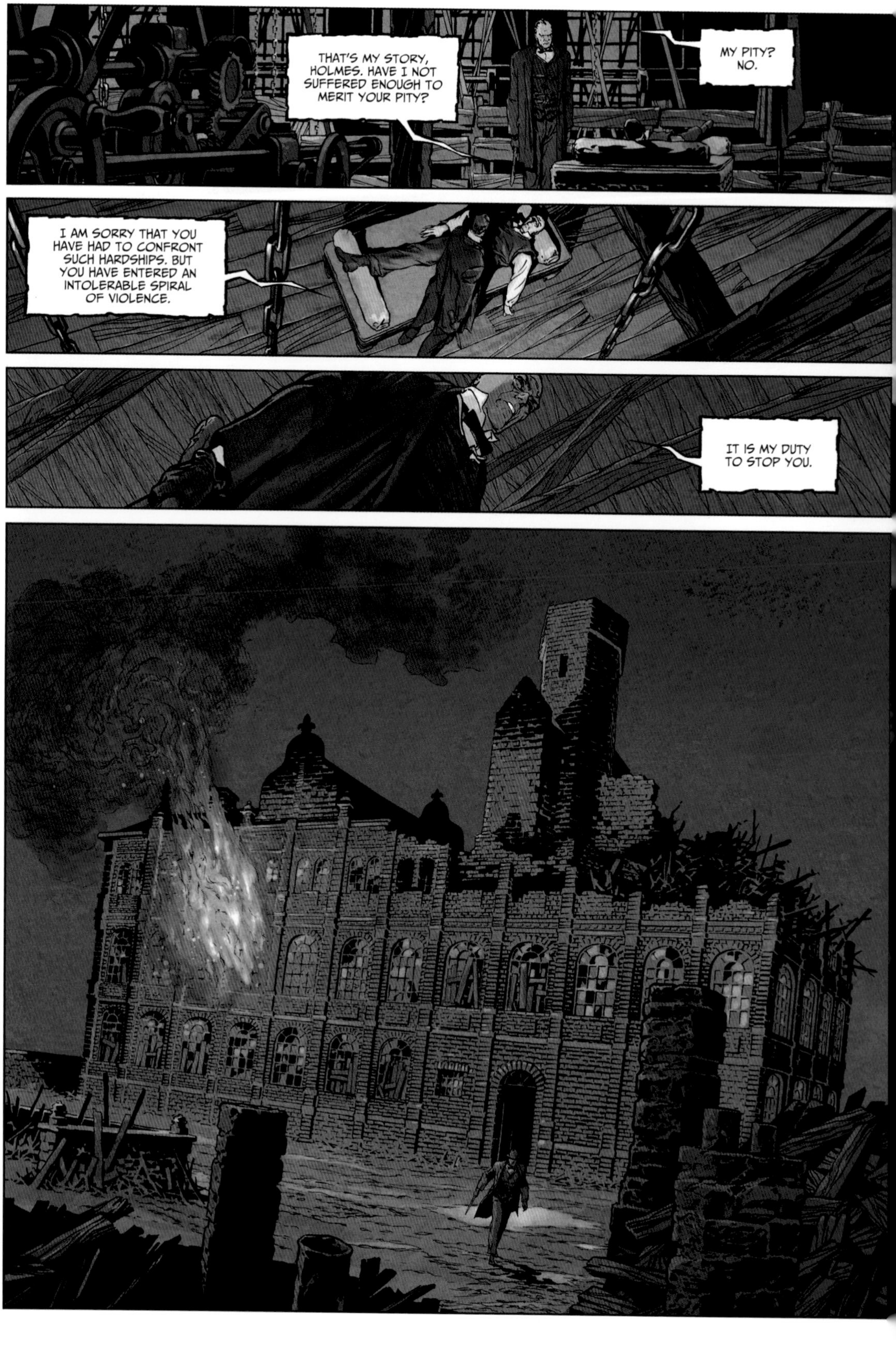
THAT'S MY STORY, HOLMES. HAVE I NOT SUFFERED ENOUGH TO MERIT YOUR PITY?
MY PITY? NO.
I AM SORRY THAT YOU HAVE HAD TO CONFRONT SUCH HARDSHIPS. BUT YOU HAVE ENTERED AN INTOLERABLE SPIRAL OF VIOLENCE.
IT IS MY DUTY TO STOP YOU.

YOU'RE LUCKY THAT I FREED MYSELF BEFORE DAYBREAK.

I DIDN'T HAVE THE CHOICE... YOU WOULD HAVE TAKEN ME BACK TO SELYMES ONCE CHANES HAD BEEN ELIMINATED, AND I'VE GOT BUSINESS TO SETTLE BEFORE GIVING MYSELF UP TO HIM...

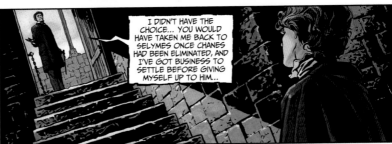

LOOK AT THE POSITIVE SIDE OF THE SITUATION: YOU CAN NOW GIVE THE GOOD NEWS TO YOUR MASTER.

I WILL LET HIM KNOW, WITHIN A FEW DAYS, WHERE HE CAN FIND ME AND, ACCORDING TO OUR ARRANGEMENT, HE CAN DISPOSE OF ME.

ON THE OTHER HAND IF, IN BETWEEN TIMES, HE TOUCHES A SINGLE HAIR OF THE WATSONS, HIS SECRETS WILL BECOME PUBLIC...

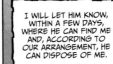

YOU WILL PAY FOR THIS!

THERE YOU ARE, MY OLD FRIEND. YOU KNOW ALL.

BY LETTING PEOPLE BELIEVE I HAD DISAPPEARED, I THOUGHT TO PROTECT YOU. I WAS WRONG.

NIGHT IS COMING...

I COULD NOT STOP SELYMES FROM ATTACKING YOUR WIFE. BUT BE ASSURED THAT I WON'T LET HIM COME NEAR YOU AGAIN, EVEN IF I HAVE TO SACRIFICE MY LIFE FOR IT.

I GIVE YOU THIS BOOK FOR SAFE-KEEPING. CONSIDER IT AS MY WILL AND TESTAMENT.

WHEN YOU HAVE READ IT, GIVE IT TO MYCROFT AND DON'T TALK TO ANYONE ELSE.

SOME STORIES CAN'T BE SHARED EVEN WITH THOSE CLOSE TO US. IT'S BETTER THAT MARY DOESN'T KNOW OF WHAT MONSTER SHE WAS THE PREY.

IT WAS AN HONOR TO KNOW YOU, WATSON. MAY THE FUTURE GIVE YOU ITS BEST.

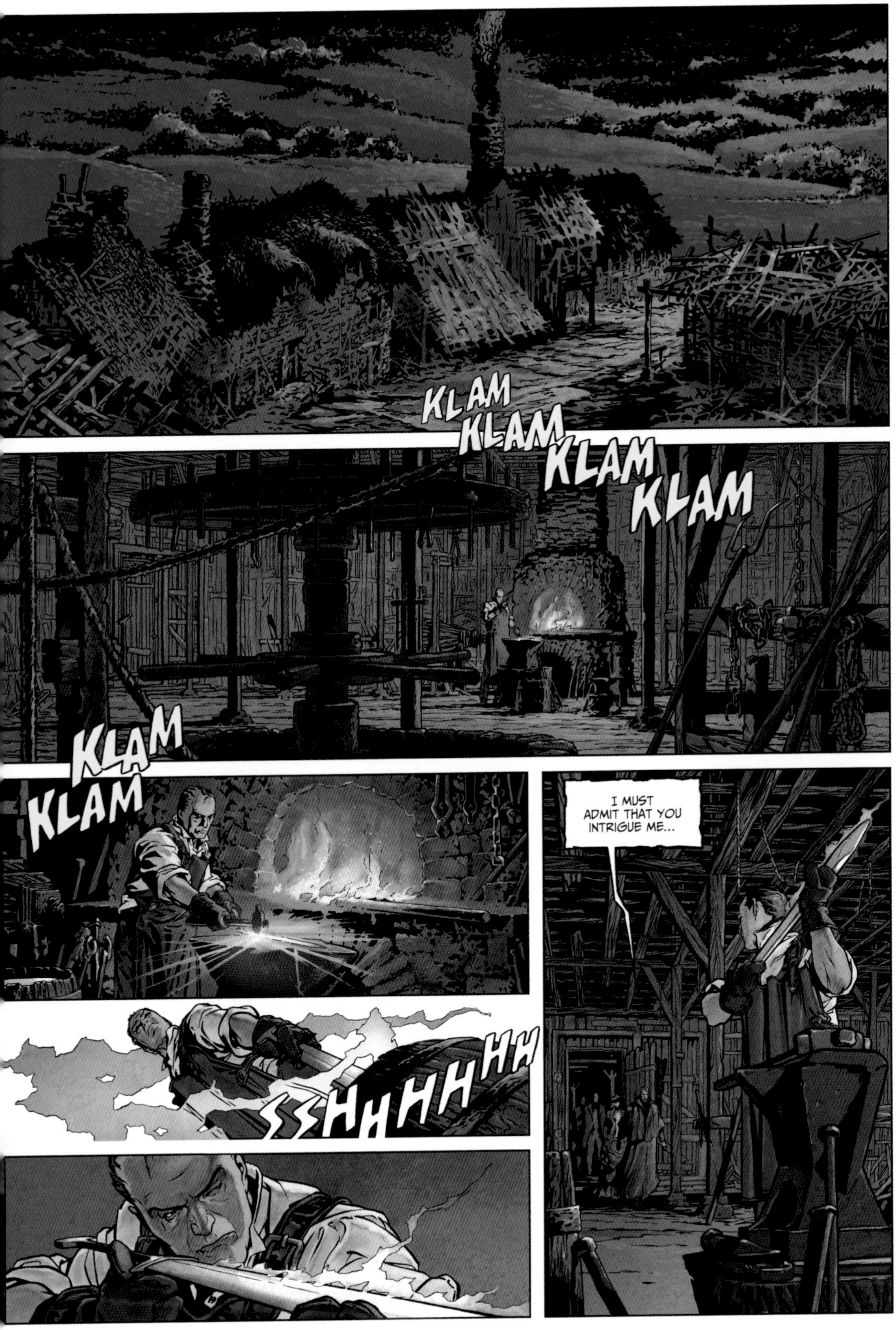
KLAM
KLAM
KLAM
KLAM
KLAM
KLAM
I MUST ADMIT THAT YOU INTRIGUE ME...
SSHHHHHHH

WHEN JOYCE TOLD ME HOW YOU TRICKED HER, I THOUGHT YOU WERE GOING TO DISAPPEAR.

UNTIL I RECEIVED YOUR INVITATION.

WHY CHOOSE THIS PLACE?

I HAVE FOND MEMORIES...

MY FAMILY LIVED LESS THAN A MILE FROM HERE AND GOT SUPPLIES FROM THE FARM. AS I WAS A CURIOUS CHILD AND LIKED BY THE OWNERS, THEY TAUGHT ME ABOUT THEIR DAILY LIVES.

IT IS IN THIS FORGE THAT I LEARNT PATIENCE, A CERTAIN SENSE OF METHOD, SATISFACTION OF A JOB WELL DONE... QUALITIES WHICH SERVED ME WHEN I BECAME INTERESTED IN THE VIOLIN AND THEN CHEMISTRY.

IF EVERYTHING SHOULD FINISH, IT'S BETTER TO BE HERE.

YOU ENVISAGE YOUR END VERY SERENELY.

I HAVE PREPARED MYSELF.

FOR DEATH PERHAPS, BUT NOT FOR JOYCE'S REVENGE...

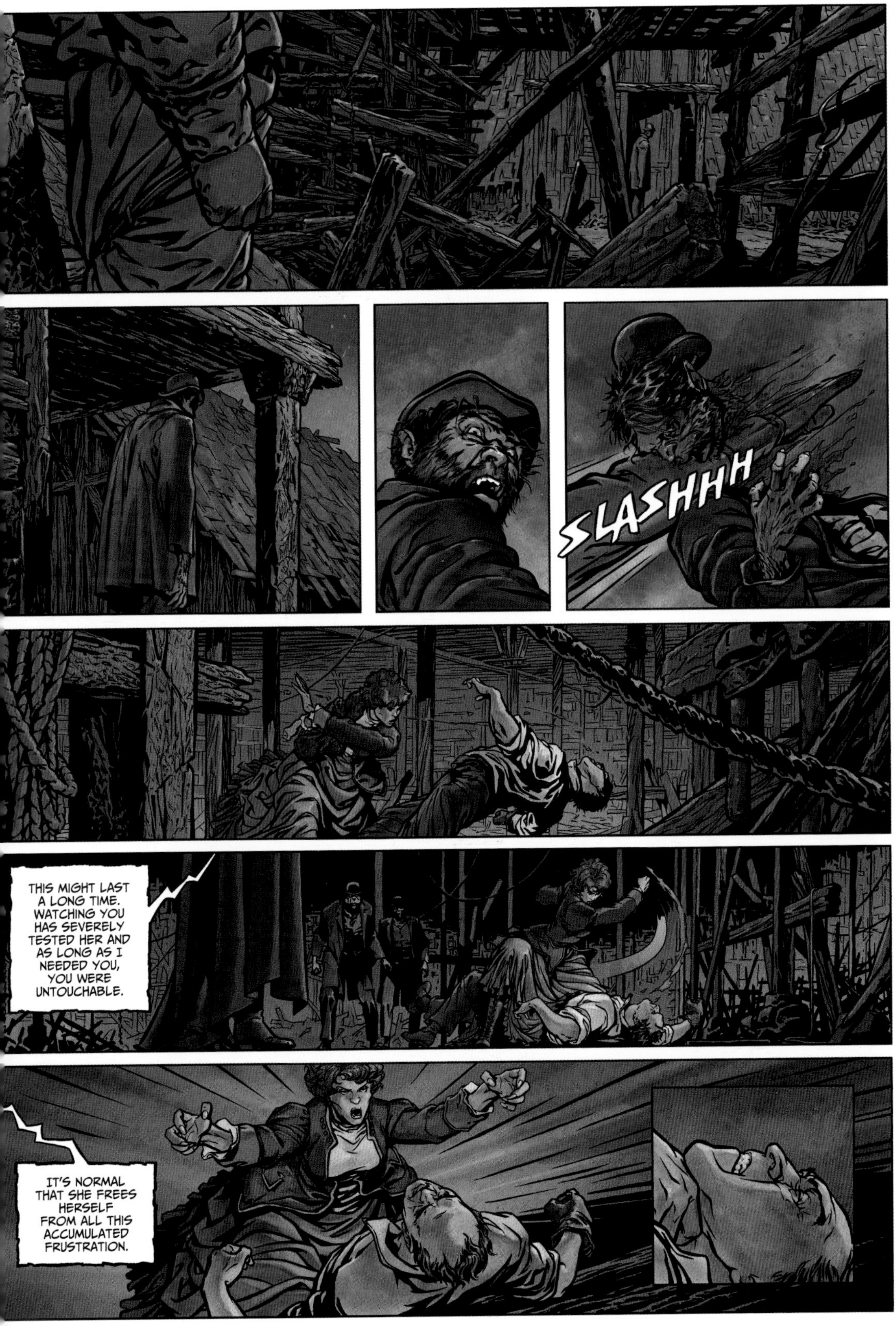

SLASHHH
THIS MIGHT LAST A LONG TIME. WATCHING YOU HAS SEVERELY TESTED HER AND AS LONG AS I NEEDED YOU, YOU WERE UNTOUCHABLE.
IT'S NORMAL THAT SHE FREES HERSELF FROM ALL THIS ACCUMULATED FRUSTRATION.

I PROMISED YOU, HOLMES! IT'S TIME TO SETTLE OUR DIFFERENCES!

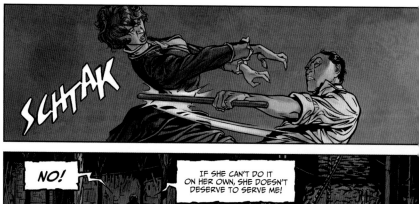

SCHTAK

NO!

IF SHE CAN'T DO IT ON HER OWN, SHE DOESN'T DESERVE TO SERVE ME!

IS SHE ALSO OF YOUR BLOOD, SELYMES?

I DO BELIEVE IT. LUCKILY, I HAVE BETTER ARGUMENTS...

CRAKK

I CAN RENDER YOU A SERVICE AND GET RID OF HER BEFORE MADNESS TAKES HOLD OF HER.

YOU ARE HOPING TO GET OUT OF THINGS BY DIVIDING US? THAT WILL NOT SAVE YOU...

FLOSHHH

THIS GROTESQUE DISGUISE... IS IT SERIOUS?

HOLMES ISN'T REPUTED FOR HIS FANTASY.

CHANES?

KILL HIM!

AS FOR YOU, I SHALL BREAK YOUR BONES ONE AFTER THE OTHER FOR MISSING ME!

NO, SELYMES, YOU WON'T DO ANY MORE HARM!

I DIDN'T MAKE THE CONNECTION IMMEDIATELY... I HAD TO SEE THE LIGHTNING CLOSE TO ME TO UNDERSTAND.

THE REASON WHY YOU HAVE NO PHOTOS OF OWEN CHANES... YOU VAMPIRES FEAR PHOTOFLASHES!

I WANT YOU TO KNOW... WHEN WE'VE FINISHED HERE, NOTHING WILL REMAIN OF YOU.

WITH THIS REVELATION, I STUDIED THE PRODUCTION OF MAGNESIUM FLASH POWDER. CAVERS USE SACHETS LIKE THESE TO PHOTOGRAPH GROTTOES. MAGNESIUM AND BENGAL PAPER... DANGEROUS BUT EFFICIENT.

I'M SURE THAT YOU BETTER UNDERSTAND THE USE OF THE DIVING SUIT. IT ALLOWED CHANES TO MASK HIS SMELL.

HOLMES...

CHANES WROTE A LETTER TO QUEEN VICTORIA. HE HAS PROMISED TO STOP HIS SERIES OF CRIMES AND TO KILL YOU.

THAT YOUR CASTLE AND YOUR FAITHFUL SERVANTS BE DELIVERED TO THE FLAMES...

TONIGHT, PRECISELY.

YOU CONCEITED IDIOT! DO YOU BELIEVE THAT YOU CAN SURVIVE AFTER THROWING THAT IN MY FACE?

I SHALL MAKE YOU ETERNAL, HOLMES! AND I SHALL TORMENT YOU UNTIL THE END OF TIME!

TONK

TONK

I'M NOT FORGETTING YOU, OWEN!

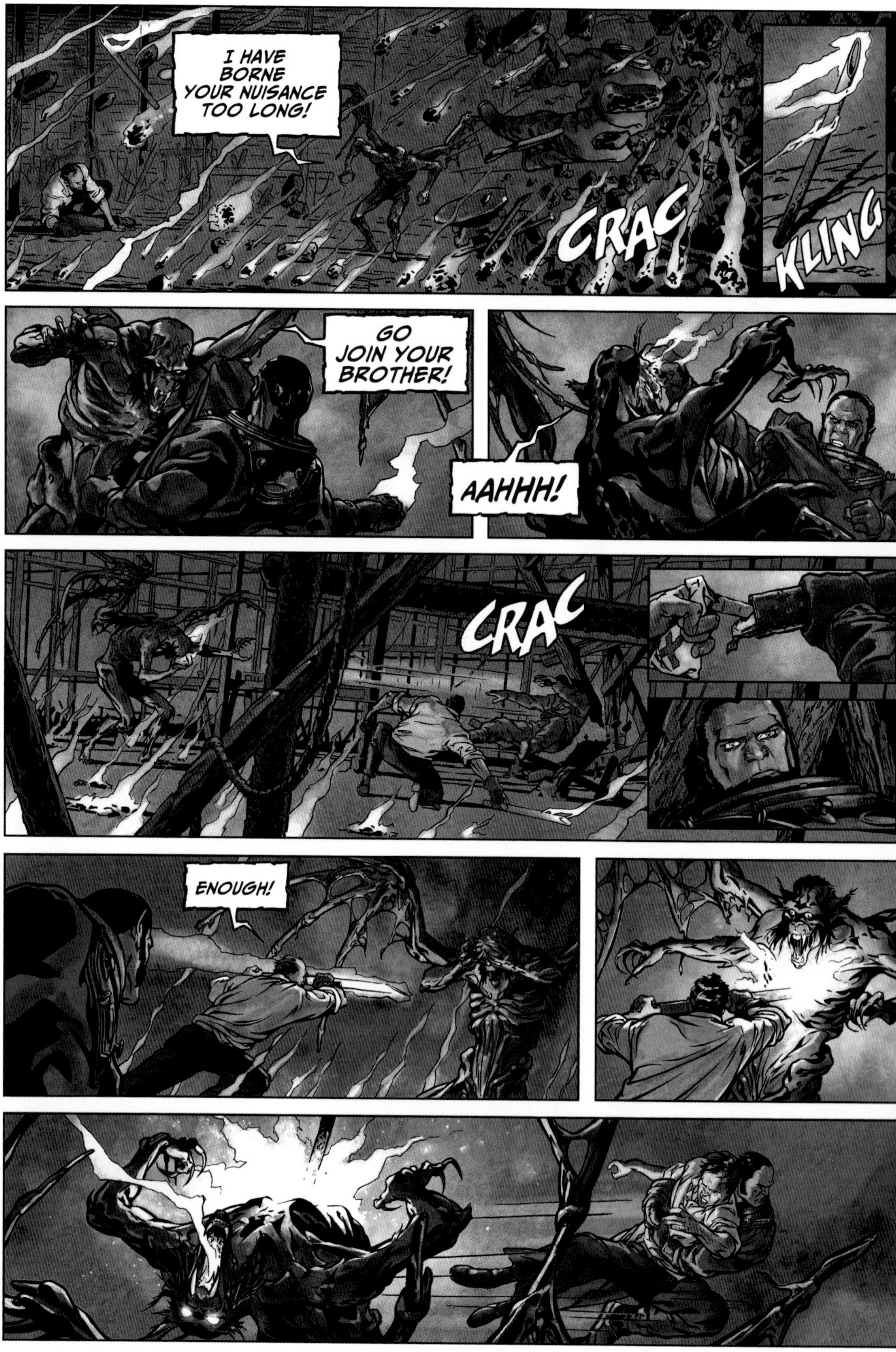
I HAVE BORNE YOUR NUISANCE TOO LONG!
CRAC
KLING
GO JOIN YOUR BROTHER!
AAHHH!
CRAC
ENOUGH!

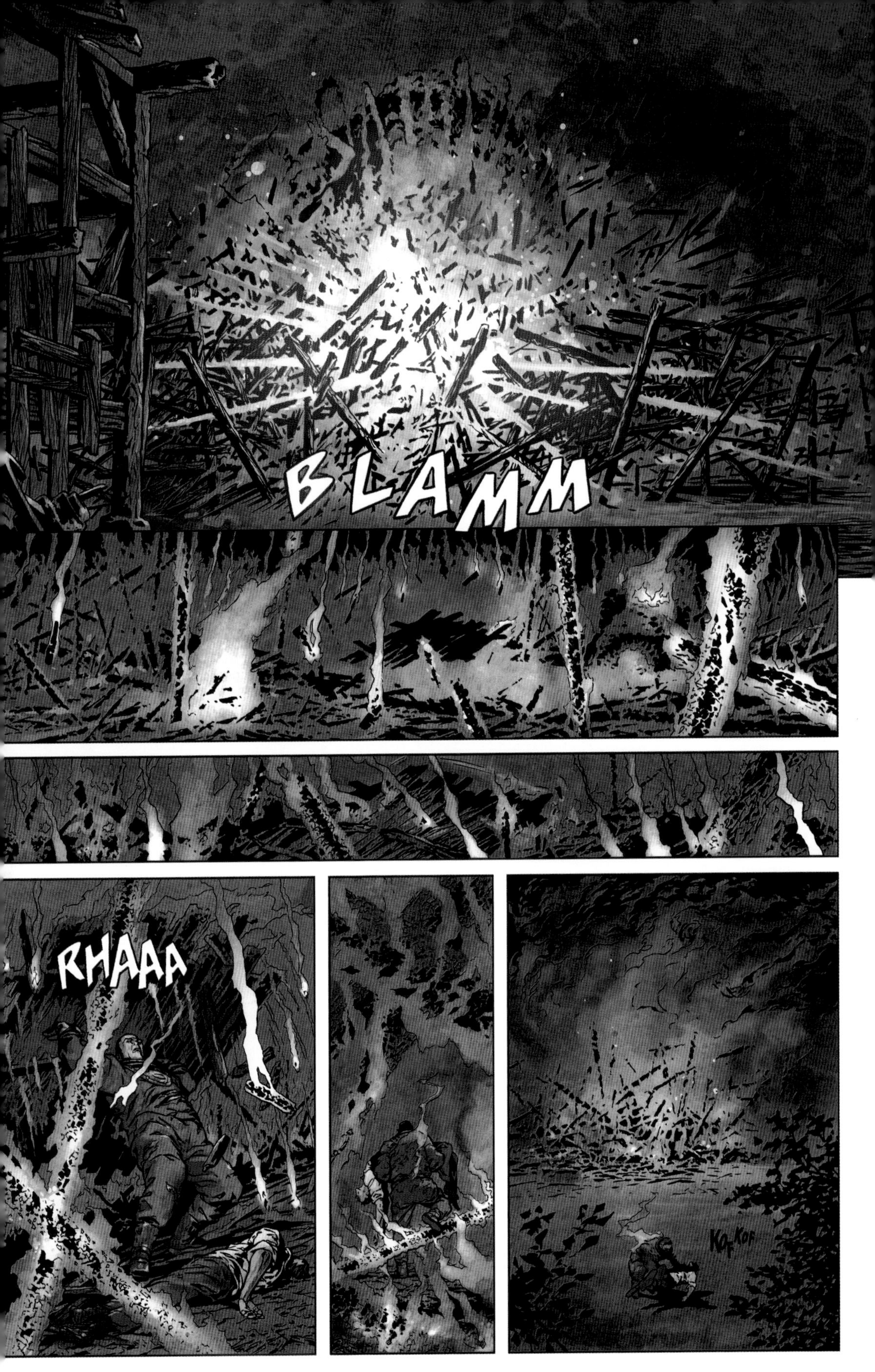
BLAMM
RHAAA
KOF KOF

THOSE SACHETS THAT YOU USED AGAINST SELYMES... IT WAS RATHER AN EXPLOSIVE MIXTURE.

I UNDERSTOOD WHEN I SAW THE RED MARKS.

YOU WANTED TO BE SURE THAT WE'D ALL BE KILLED. IT'S A PITY I'M SO SWIFT...

I SUPPOSE THAT THAT ENDS OUR AGREEMENT.

I COULDN'T LET YOU GO.

YOU WILL KILL FOR BLOOD... EVEN FOR PLEASURE.

BECAUSE I'M A MONSTER.

AND MONSTERS HAVE TO BE KILLED, DON'T THEY?

I CAN'T HOLD IT AGAINST YOU. IN YOUR EYES, WE ARE ALL ALIKE. IN A CERTAIN WAY, YOU ARE RIGHT...

I COULD HAVE LET YOU DIE IN THIS INFERNO. I DIDN'T.

JUST AS I'M RESISTING THE OVERWHELMING IDEA OF TEARING OFF YOUR HEAD.

I'M STRUGGLING EVERY MINUTE NOT TO YIELD TO MY URGES. I'M TRYING TO TAME THE ANIMAL WITHIN ME.

HOW?

YOUR EXPERIENCE WITH DRUGS.

WITHOUT MORPHINE ACETATE, I WOULD BE AT THE MERCY OF MY INSTINCTS. BUT IT'S ONLY A STOPGAP. YOU CAN OFFER ME BETTER.

YOU SAVED MY LIFE WHEN I WAS A CHILD. I'M NOW ASKING YOU TO SAVE MY SOUL.

OF COURSE, I DIDN'T BELIEVE IN HIS SINCERITY FOR A SECOND. BUT I WAS NOT OF A SIZE TO CONFRONT HIM. I HAD TO GAIN TIME...

THE OCCASION WAS NOT LONG IN PRESENTING ITSELF...

AFTER OUR VICTORY OVER SELYMES, CHANES AND I WENT BACK TO LONDON.

I RECOVERED SLOWLY FROM THE COMBAT AND WAS DRAWING UP A PLAN TO ELIMINATE HIM WHEN HE GAVE ME HIS HEAD ON A PLATE.

TO PROVE HIS GOOD FAITH, HE CHOSE TO WEAR FETTERS AND TO REMAIN UNDER MY SURVEILLANCE UNTIL I DEVELOPED A COCKTAIL GUARANTEEING HIS TEMPERANCE.

I COULD NOT HOPE FOR BETTER. HOWEVER... HE GAVE ME ALL CONTROL OVER HIM, AFTER ASKING FOR MY HELP.

I DON'T NEED ANYONE TO REMIND ME HOW MUCH VAMPIRES ARE ABJECT AND DEMONIACAL CREATURES.

MEN'S JUSTICE COULD NOT BE APPLIED TO HIM. HIS SURVIVAL THEREFORE DEPENDED ON ME ONLY. EITHER I IGNORED HIS EFFORTS AND SENT HIM TO HELL, OR I HELPED HIM.

BUT I ALSO KNOW THAT THE WORST INDIVIDUALS CAN VANQUISH THEIR DEMONS IF THEY ARE DETERMINED TO DO SO. CHANES SHOWED HIS DETERMINATION AND TOOK THE RISK OF RENDERING HIMSELF VULNERABLE.

THERE IS ONE THING I BELIEVE IN: THE HUMANE SIDE OF A CRIMINAL, HOWEVER HARDENED HE BE, DESERVES TO BE CULTIVATED. AFTER A LONG PERIOD OF REFLECTION, IT WAS THIS PRECISE POINT THAT MADE MY DECISION.

IT ONLY TOOK ME A FEW DAYS TO FIND THE COMBINATION OF SUBSTANCES TO HELP CHANES.

THEN HE LEFT FOR THE AMERICAN CONTINENT. AN EXAMPLE THAT I WASN'T LONG IN FOLLOWING, APART FROM THE DESTINATION.

HE EASED MY TASK Y TESTING EACH OF MY PREPARATIONS. A SOMEWHAT MPIRICAL METHOD, T I DIDN'T HAVE TO ORRY ABOUT THE NOXIOUSNESS OF HE PRODUCTS ON IS PERSON... AND HAT SATISFIED HIS IMPATIENCE.

I TAUGHT HIM HOW TO PREPARE THE MIXTURE THAT HE'D HAVE TO INJECT INTO HIMSELF FOR THE REST OF HIS LIFE.

LEAVING LONDON WAS THE BEST WAY OF PROTECTING YOU FROM MORIARTY'S MEN, WATSON. SHERLOCK HOLMES WAS DEAD, AND SHOULD REMAIN SO.

I INVESTED PART OF MY FORTUNE IN COFINANCING A SCIENTIFIC EXPLORATION VOYAGE. MY CONTRIBUTION GAVE ME THE RIGHT TO PARTICIPATE IN THE EXPEDITION.

I WILL TELL YOU ABOUT IT... IN THE BOOK I RECOVERED FROM THE COVINGTON INN.

FINALLY, THE WILL HAS BECOME A COLLECTION OF MEMOIRS WHICH, I MUST ADMIT, SUITS ME QUITE WELL.

FRESH WHARF, LONDON BRIDGE.

MR. SIGERSON.

DR. CRAWLEY... AM I EARLY?

MORE THAN EVER.

WE WEIGH ANCHOR IN LESS THAN AN HOUR. THAT WILL LEAVE YOU THE TIME TO GET USED TO YOUR LITTLE CABIN.

READY FOR THE ADVENTURE?

THE END

ALSO FROM DARK HORSE BOOKS

JEREMIAH OMNIBUS VOLUME 1
Hermann
One of Europe's most revered comics classics comes to America! At the end of the twentieth century, the United States is overcome by race hatred, and the ensuing civil war leaves only a few million survivors and a shattered society. Forced by circumstances into a series of violent moral compromises, innocent Jeremiah and his cynical friend Kurdy attempt to find their place in the postapocalyptic world without descending into savagery.

978-1-59582-945-0 | $24.99

THE MANARA LIBRARY VOLUME 1
Milo Manara with Hugo Pratt
The first of nine volumes, The Manara Library Volume 1 collects two of Manara's seminal works in a magnificently appointed, deluxe hardcover edition. The sweeping epic Indian Summer, a collaboration with celebrated creator Hugo Pratt, is collected here along with Manara's The Paper Man, both translated by Euro comics expert Kim Thompson.

978-1-59582-782-1 | $59.99

THE INCREDIBLE ADVENTURES OF DOG MENDONÇA AND PIZZABOY
Filipe Melo and Juan Cavia
What do an overweight Portuguese werewolf, a seven-year-old girl who's actually a six thousand-year-old demon, and a downtrodden pizza boy have in common? In this smash-hit import, the unlikely team bands together to ward off occult evils, Nazis, and impending global doom! Featuring an introduction by An American Werewolf in London director John Landis!

978-1-59582-938-2 | $12.99

THE WEDNESDAY CONSPIRACY
Sergio Bleda
Think you've got problems? Meet the patients in Dr. Burton's Wednesday afternoon support group: Violet carries a jar of demons. Roger can read minds. Akiko talks with her dead parents through the bathroom mirror. Joe is an exorcist. Brian is pyrokinetic. And then, of course, there's Charles. They've been thrown together by the luck of the draw, stuck with supernatural powers they don't want and can't control. But when something begins to pick them off one by one, the surviving members of the Wednesday Conspiracy find themselves the last, reluctant line of defense between the reincarnation of an ancient evil and the fate of the world.

978-1-59582-563-6 | $19.99

MORE EUROPEAN INTRIGUE FROM

DARK HORSE BOOKS

BLACKSAD

BLACKSAD

Juan Díaz Canales and Juanjo Guarnido

The *Blacksad* books first took Europe by storm in 2000 and sold over 200,000 copies in France alone. Now Dark Horse Comics presents the beautifully painted stories of private investigator John Blacksad, up to his feline ears in mystery, digging into the backstories behind murders, child abductions, and nuclear secrets.

Volume 1
978-1-59582-393-9 | $29.99
Volume 2: A Silent Hell
978-1-59582-931-3 | $19.99

VAMPIRE BOY
CARLOS TRILLO
EDUARDO RISSO

VAMPIRE BOY

Carlos Trillo and Eduardo Risso

Left nameless by his father and sentenced to eternal life by a trick of fate and fortune, the protagonist of Carlos Trillo and Eduardo Risso's *Vampire Boy* has spent fifty centuries in a body that never ages, locked in an eternal struggle with a rival as immortal as he. Acclaimed writer Carlos Trillo teams with legendary artist Eduardo Risso (100 Bullets) to produce a poignantly engrossing twist on the classic vampire mythos, now presented in English for the first time!

978-1-59582-562-9 | $24.99

THE DYLAN DOG CASE FILES

THE DYLAN DOG CASE FILES

Tiziano Sclavi and others

Unavailable in English for almost a decade, one of the most popular comics in the world—selling more than a million copies every month throughout Europe—returns! An ex-cop who now battles against evil as a "nightmare investigator," Dylan Dog is unlike any private eye you've ever met. If creatures from beyond the unknown are after you, and if you can hire him, he just might save your life.

978-1-59582-206-2 | $24.99

DRAGONERO

DRAGONERO

Luca Enoch, Stefano Vietti, and Giuseppe Matteoni

Beyond the civilized lands of Erondàr, the Stone Towers are crumbling. The great monoliths are falling one after another under the wild thrusts of an evil force. The Ancient Prohibition that binds the Abominables inside their dark world is soon to be broken. Alben the Wizard will send for Myrva, a young follower of the powerful Technocrats; he will choose Ecuba, the fighting nun, to protect him; and he will call back Ian Aranill, a former Empire officer—followed by Gmor the Orc, his loyal friend—to use his scouting experience. Together they will face the Painers, the evil beings who still live in the barren Dragonlands. Can Ian prevail against the last, horrible threat they will be facing?

978-1-59582-291-8 | $19.99

AVAILABLE AT YOUR LOCAL COMICS SHOP OR BOOKSTORE! • To find a comics shop in your area, call 1-888-266-4226.
For more information or to order direct visit DarkHorse.com or call 1-800-862-0052 Mon.–Fri. 9 AM to 5 PM Pacific Time. Prices and availability subject to change without notice.

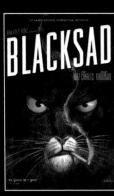